D1259683

nappy edges

nappy edges*

ntozake shange

st. martin's press/ new york

*the roots of your hair/ what
turns back when we sweat, run,
make love, dance, get afraid, get
happy: the tell-tale sign of living/

NAPPY EDGES. Copyright © 1972, 1974, 1975, 1976, 1977, 1978 by Ntozake Shange
All rights reserved. No part of this book may be used or reproduced in any
manner whatsoever without written permission except in the case of brief
quotations embodied in critical articles or reviews.
For information, write: St. Martin's Press
175 Fifth Avenue, New York, N.Y. 10010
Printed in the United States of America

Library of Congress Cataloging in Publication Data
Shange, Ntozake.
Nappy edges*
"*The roots of your hair/what turns back when we
sweat, run, make love, dance, get afraid, get happy:
the tell-tale signs of living."
I. Title.
PS3569.H3324N3   811'.5'4   78-3001
ISBN 0-312-06424-1

Some of the pieces
in this book originally appeared in Yardbird Reader, Bopp, Viva, Anon,
Mademoiselle,
Mosaic, Invisible City, Pacifica Journal, Black Maria, Ms.,
The Next World, and the Shameless Hussy Press
edition of for colored girls who have considered suicide/
when the rainbow is enuf.

First U.S. Paperback Edition: September 1991
10 9 8 7 6 5 4 3 2 1

for
sassafrass, cypress, indigo,
graciéla & smoke
sierra, seattle, memphis
melissa, mykko, lily & trinidad
memories & hopes

& love to
ronare bearden
in all his hues

Me Go
Tule Lake.
Me Stay
Carifonia.
Home.
—Lawson Inada

all unfulfilled desires are imprisoned children
—Anais Nin

contents

things i wd say

love & other highways

closets

& she bleeds

whispers with the unicorn

nappy edges

things i wd say

. . . *from this moment forward you will learn to think*
by fighting your own language.
—Juan Goytisolo, *Juan the Landless*

It was not until 1947 that Bolo believed that the war was over. Up till that time
he used to say, "Is only a lot of propaganda, just lies for black people."
—V. S. Naipaul, *Miguel Street*

takin a solo/ a poetic possibility/ a poetic imperative

if i asked: is this james brown or clifford jordan? you wd know. if i
said: is this fletcher henderson's band or the black byrds? you wd
know. i say/ pick one: ayler or coltrane. here's another: charlie
parker or ben webster. most of you wd know. the tone. the lyric.
rhythm & cadence of the musician is a personal thing to you. you lis-
ten & learn the particular flow of a particular somebody.

soon you'll say: that's oliver lake. not julius hemphill. or that cdnt be
david murray. that's gotta be hamiett bluiett. you cd go so far as to
say joseph jarman wd never play anything like that. or even point
ornette coleman out/ shd you see him in any where/ & say . . . he
is history.

we can do this with any kinda horn . . . clarinets, saxophones,
trumpets/ tell me what does 'some day my prince will come'/ mean
to you. that is not snow white or walt disney/ that is miles davis.
some of us can even differentiate mongo santamaria from pablo 'po-
tato' valdes and ray barretto from johnny pacheko. others can pick
ron carter from a segway of mingus & hopkins & favors. we hear so
well/ remember solos that were improvisations/ we are thoroughly
smitten by the nature of the thing/ if we talk abt music.

you never doubt bessie smith's voice. i cd not say to you: that's
chaka khan singin 'empty bed blues'. not cuz chaka khan cant sing
empty bed blues/ but cuz bessie smith sounds a certain way. her
way. if tina turner stood right here next to me & simply said
'yes' . . . we wd all know/ no matter how much i love her/ no mat-
ter what kinda wig-hat i decide to wear/ my 'yes' will never be tina's
'yes'. and that's what i want to discuss with you this evening.

we, as a people, or as a literary cult, or a literary culture/ have not demanded singularity from our writers. we cd all sound the same. come from the same region. be the same gender. born the same year. & though none of the above is true, a black writer can get away with/ abscond & covet for him or herself/ the richness of his or her person/ long before a black musician or singer cd.

now why is this? we don't understand the beauty of language? that cant be true. according to dillard & smith we make up a good part of contemporary american language/ on our own/ cd it be we assume a collaboration with any blk writer/ who attempts to re-create blk english/ blk culture/ cuz that's ours. we were there. we know abt that. & that poet/ that novelist/ that playwrite/ happened to be there at the time/ when some other somebody just like me/ waz sayin or doin/ exactly what i say & do. that means there is absolutely no acceptance of blk personal reality. if you are 14, female & black in the u.s.a./ you have one solitary voice/ though you number 3 million/ no nuance exists for you/ you have been sequestered in the monolith/ the common denominator as persona. what i am getting to is the notion that as a people we have so claimed 'the word'/ we dont even pay attention to who is speakin. is this leroi jones:

> who will know what I am and what I wanted beneath the maze
> of memories and attitudes that shape the reality of everything.
> Beneath the necessity of talking or the necessity for being
> angry and beneath the actual core of life we make reference to
> digging deep into some young woman, and listening to her
> come.

or imamu baraka?

we do not need to be fucked with
we can be quiet and think and love the silence
we need to look at trees more closely
we need to listen

there's a difference/ in syntax, imagery, rhythm & theme. who is
this: bob kaufman or david henderson, or thulani or papoleto melen-
dez or me:

i pick a plume & let you have it
what you see is what you get
if you limit yrself—you lose—

that's the division of a realm bordered by bebop & one sunk in sylla-
ble/ where only the language defines reality. we have poets who
speak to you of elephants & avenues/ we have others who address
themselves to worlds having no existence beyond the word. that's
fine. we live all those places. but, if we don't know the voice of a
writer/ the way we know 'oh . . . that's trane'/ something is very
wrong. we are unfortunately/ sellin ourselves down the river again.
& we awready know abt that. if we go down river again/ just cuz we
don't know or care to recognize our particularities/ wont nobody
come/ cuz dont nobody care/ if you dont know yr poets as well as
yr tenor horns.

you dont resist count basie cuz he's from red bank. i never heard of
any one disparaging eric dolphy for bein born & raised in los an-
geles/ is anybody mad at miles davis cus his father was a doctor/
nobody is peeved at pacheco cuz he is from the dominican republic/
but i can tell you who is a poet from chicago/ i cd say that's some

4/

west coast stuff/ or some new york number/ & there will be a great noddin of heads & uh-huhs/ cuz we dont ask a poet to speak personally/ we want a poet to talk like an arena/ or like a fire station/ to be everywhere/ all at once/ even if we never been there/ but especially if we've never been there/ we expect a poet to clear a space/ not her space/ not a secret/ not a closed room/ but the town. we assume the poet to be the voice of everywhere we are not/ as opposed to bein 'everything we are'. though what authentic musical criticism of our artists that exists/ always allows them the space to be themselves. a.b. spellman did not write a book callt/ bebop. he wrote a book called/ *four lives in the bebop business.* in *black music/* leroi jones demanded only that each 'apple core'/ be singular/ be, in this case, himself (though that had more to do with circumstance than sexism).

my basic premise is that poets address themselves to the same issues as musicians/ but that we give the musicians more space to run with/ more personal legitimacy than we give our writers. here is a series of poems & compositions that approach the same themes/ if not the same themes they approach the same energy levels/ if not the same energy levels/ they approach the same rhythmic offensive/ as sun ra's version of *take the a train:* ishmael reed:

> *i am a cowboy in the boat of ra*
> *varmoosed from the temple i bedded*
> *down with Isis, Lady of the Boogaloo, dove*
> *down deep in her horny stuck up her Well*
> *Far-agao in daring midday get away.*
> *'start grabbing the blue'*
> *i said from atop my double crown.*

5/

or take victor hernandez-cruz' doing poetry:

> the poet sees & hears the world.
> & there are many worlds.
> people live in different worlds
> got different bags
> humans talk
> dance & make noise
> a poet must make poetry out of that
> or make poetry out of his mind
> which took form in the world.
> words & music travel.
> god would not make anything bad or dirty.
> some people make dirty things happen tho.
> i see what's in the world & sing it like a god.

& give the rest to dolphy. there is no incongruence here. but you wd know dolphy & maybe not hernandez-cruz. here/ compare leroi jones with himself as baraka:

> seeing no one. not wanting anyone. but you all.
> i want now to have all your minds.
> want now, to be them.

here is another nuance of baraka/ beautiful black women:

> Beautiful black women, fail, they act.
> Stop them, raining.
> They are so beautiful, we want them with us.
> Stop them raining.

6/

Beautiful, stop raining, they fail.
We fail them & their lips stick out perpetually, at our
  weakness.
Raining. Stop them.
Black queens, Ruby Dee weeps at the window, raining, being
  lost in her life,
Being what we all will be, sentimental
Bitter frustrated, deprived of her fullest light.
Beautiful black women, it is still raining
In this terrible land.

as so often assumed by academicians/ the work as leroi jones does
not overshadow the work of imamu technically. now/ hear david
murray's *flowers for albert* & know that sorrows or incantations may
be as gentle as they are grieving/ as lyrical as they are abandoned to
despair. here/ clarence major/ *reflex & bone structure:*

> *on the wall is an edward hopper painting of an all night diner.*
> *the loneliness kills me. they bury me in atlanta. cora invited*
> *shirley macclaine & marcello mastroianni to the funeral but*
> *they don't show. a lot of colored writers send flowers.*

imagine the opening speech in adrienne kennedy's *rat's mask*
(brother rat) with albert ayler's *ghosts:*

> *Kay within our room I see our dying baby,*
> *Nazis screaming girls & cursing boys, empty*
> *swings, a dark sun. There are worms in the*
> *attic beams. They scream and say we are damned.*
> *I see dying and grey cats walking.*

Kay within our room I see a dying baby, Nazis,
again they scream and say we are damned.
Within our once capital I see us dying.

here is gylan kain's *love song number 33* which merges with julius
hemphill's *hard blues* music:

we make love in the burning tenement
my knife
upon your womb
fingers upon your neck/ you scream
black satin woman
you are the boston strangler turned in upon yr self
i am not the man who kicked you
down the endless shaft of stairs
i am the black flute
yr vulva lips refused to play.

or compare bob kaufman's *song of the broken giraffe* with the sound
of oliver lake's *altoviolin* or roscoe mitchell's *nonaah*:

I continued to love despite all the traffic light difficulties
In most cases, a sane hermit will beat a good big man.
We waited in vain for the forest fire, but the bus was late
all night we baked the government into a big mud pie.
Not one century passed without shakespeare calling us dirty
    names
with all those syllables, we couldn't write a cheerful death
    notice.

> The man said *we could have a birthday party, if we*
> *surrendered.*
> *Their soldiers refused to wear evening gowns on guard duty*
> *those men in the basement were former breakfast food*
> *salesmen*
> *we hadda choice of fantasies, but naturally we were*
> *greedy . . .*
> *at the moment of truth we were dancing a minuet and missed*
> *out.*

kaufman's voice is quite like muhal richard abrams' 1 & 4 plus 2 & 7. we assume the tune or the composition is the person/ is the reality the tune is. we assume a poet has no grounding/ the poem can float in the air & belong to all of us/ long as we deny the individuality of the word. the specificity of language cd allow us so much more. i suggest that thulani is quite as incisive as the art ensemble of chicago/ in *people in sorrow*:

> *with closed lips & knotted secrets/ choke the speech/*
> *cut the throat/ cut the throat behind the veil*
> *the rich phantasma. wanted not taken*
> *the nightmare & the dream*
> *if you ask for me/ i'm never there*
> *i hide in the streets*

until we believe in the singularity of our persons/ our spaces, language & therefore craft, will not be nurtured consciously. our writers will come across it/ if they want. but we won't recognize it/ cuz like i said is this conyus:

the way of the new world is endless, imposing & present
there is a different reality that i cannot recognize
in the living nor dead; the earth is moist with them
& below the vastness of the backwater
lie drummed skinned boys collapsed in silence.

or jessica hagedorn:

sometimes you remind me of lady day
& i tell you sadness
the weariness in yr eyes/ the walk you have
kinda brave when you swing yr hips
sometimes serenity in yr eyes
& the love always.

i know you know the difference tween elvin jones & tony williams. if you take us as seriously as you take a set of traps/ a saxophone/ maybe we'll have decades of poems you'll never forget.

we assume a musical solo is a personal statement/ we think the poet is speakin for the world. there's something wrong there, a writer's first commitment is to the piece, itself. how the words fall & leap/ or if they dawdle & sit down fannin themselves. writers are dealin with language/ not politics. that comes later. so much later. to think abt the politics of a poem/ before we think abt the poem/ is to put what is correct before the moment. if the moment waz not correct/ it still waz. we dont castigate ornette coleman for 'lonely woman'/ nor do we chastise the del vikings for singing abt love all the time. we accept what they gave us/ cuz that's what they had & it waz good.

10/

when i take my voice into a poem or a story/ i am trying desperately
to give you that. i am not trying to give you a history of my family/
the struggle of black people all over the world or the fight goin on
upstairs tween susie & matt. i am givin you a moment/ like some-
thing that isnt coming back/ something particularly itself/ like an
alto solo in december in nashville in 1937.

as we demand to be heard/ we want you to hear us. we come to you
the way leroi jenkins comes or cecil taylor/ or b.b. king. we come to
you alone/ in the theater/ in the story/ & the poem. like with billie
holiday or betty carter/ we shd give you a moment that cannot be
re-created/ a specificity that cannot be confused. our language shd
let you know who's talkin, what we're talkin abt & how we cant stop
sayin this to you. some urgency accompanies the text. something im-
portant is going on. we are speakin. reachin for yr person/ we can-
not hold it/ we dont wanna sell it/ we give you ourselves/ if you
listen.

hear thulani:

> yes the holy ghost waz fine tonight
> but i had to leave him in the place
> you see i just walked in off the street
> & i'm trying to keep a date
> i'm trying to give away what's left of me
> that aint been bought or just plain taken
> y'know i try so hard to keep ma biziness to myself.

if you listen/

hear pietri:

> *we are gathered here today to say we are gathered here today*
> *because we are not gathered somewhere else to say we are*
> *gathered here today & not somewhere else we are gathered*
> *here today because this is somewhere else & because we are*
> *not gathered somewhere else to tell you differently.*

if you listen/

hear kaufman:

> *jazz listen to it at yr own risk*
> *at the beginning, a warm dark place.*
> *. . .*
> *(her screams were trumpet's laughter*
> *not quite blues, but almost sinful*
> *crying above the pain, we forgave ourselves)*

you cd imagine us like music & make us yrs/

> *we can be quiet & think & love the silence*
> *we need to look at trees more closely*
> *we need to listen*

> *—delivered at the National*
> *Afro-American Writers Conference/*
> *Howard University, May 1977.*

wow . . . yr just like a man!

he said hangin out with her waz just like hangin out witta man/ she
cd drink & talk pungently/ even tell a risqué joke or two/ more n
that/ she cd talk abt art/ & that musta made her a man/ cuz she sure
cdnt scratch her balls/ or pee further n him/ or fuck a tiny fella in
the ass/ she didn't have a football letter/ & she cdnt talk abt how
many women she'd had/ but then we dont know that either/ all we
know is he said she waz just like a fella/ & here she waz thinkin she
waz as good as any woman/ which to her meant she waz as good as
any fella/ but that's an idea without a large following in these parts/
any way the way the relationship evolved/ he & this woman he waz
thinkin waz like a fella/ well they worked together alla the time/
had poetry readings/ did exercises/ saw shows/ cut-up everybody
else's work on the phone/ & you must know since/ she hadta be a
fella to understand/ probably you awready guessed/ their shared
craft waz poetry/ cuz words/ are a man's thing/ you know/ the
craftsmen/ the artisan/ the artist/ they are all in men/ why else wd
you haveta put 'ess' on the end of every damn thing/ if it waznt to
signify when/ a woman waz doin something that men do/

so anyway they were poets/ & this guy well he liked this woman's
work/ cuz it waznt 'personal'/ i mean a man can get personal in his
work when he talks politics or bout his dad/ but women start alla
this foolishness bout their bodies & blood & kids & what's really goin
on at home/ well & that aint poetry/ that's goo-ey gaw/ female
stuff/ & she waznt like that/ this woman they callt a poet/ wrote
mostly abt 'the music'/ ya know albert ayler/ david murray/ bobo
shaw/ olu dara/ archie shepp/ oliver lake/ she even had a whole
series for the art ensemble of chicago/ now this waz phenomenal/
cuz these were men who were poets/ were mostly into coltrane or

bebop/ not havin moved ahead with the times/ & they thot this
woman/ musta slept with alla these guys/ cuz everybody knows/
women dont really know how to listen to music/ or even what's a
gift like billie holiday/ why betty carter & vi redd were never treated
weird by musicians who were men/ they just didnt get any work/ so
this woman who waz a poet/ musta changed her ways considerably/
& the other poets liked that/ there waznt any reason/ to hold up a
readin cuz some bitch waz late gettin up from a good dickin down/
tho some poetry readings never started cuz some men who were
poets cd never get it up.

but this woman she waz alone a lot of the time with her books fulla
these crazy poems abt this wild music/ so that waz awright/ some-
body asked her one time to tell the truth/ waz she run out on her
husband/ & she laughed/ they tried to make her blood sister/ a lover
she had in the closet/ but when the mother of both the woman who
waz a poet & the sister suspected of bein a lover in the closet
showed up to a readin with the husband of the mother & the father
of the poet who waz a woman & the lover in the closet/ that rumor
cooled out/ still there waz a problem/ the poet who waz a woman
who wrote like a man faced and that waz that she waz a woman &
when the poets who were men/ were feelin fiercely good abt bein
men/ they often forgot that this waz a woman whom they all said
waz more like a man cuz she cd talk/ & she didnt write none of that
personal stuff/ they forgot they had said this/ & started to make the
wet mouth & heavy arms with her/ & she waz stunned cuz she waz
the one who had no gender to speak of cuz here she waz a woman
who waz really more like one of the fellas/ but that waz when the
fellas were bein poets/ when the fellas were bein fellas/ they didnt

14/

care if she cd talk or not/ & they sometimes didnt recognize her &
told her they met her in seattle last year at their mother's/

she waz very nice to the guys & sometimes fed them like their own
mamas wd have/ or lent them some money like a bank wda if banks
werent apriori scared to death of poets in need of money/ sometimes
when one of their women threw them out/ they stayed at her house/
cuz there waz never a man at her house/ that waz one of the unspo-
ken rules of her bein considered one of the fellas/ or a poet/ cuz if
there waz a man at her house/ like there waz one time/ when she
forgot that in order to be considered a poet she hadta be one of the
guys/ the poets who were men/ got very indignant & walked out cuz
she waz romancin some fella who waznt even a poet & wdnt be able
to feed them that night/ not that they had callt or anything/ see/
among poets who are men & women deigned poets by these men/
there is a strange/ spontaneity/ that says they cd come visit when-
ever they liked & she mustnt call cuz their ol ladies didn't under-
stand that she waz one of the fellas/ & they made it hard on any
fella who waznt a poet to be a lover of hers/ cuz they wd show up
all the time with these wounds from the police/ an irate poet/ at-
tackin the doorbell/ one had his nose broken for stealin an image &
landed up in her kitchen/ when the woman who waz a poet waz just
abt to get down to business in her bed/ & that kinda thing is hard for
a man who is not a poet to take/ plus/ they wd quiz the man who
waz not a poet abt poetry/ & since he waz not a poet & didnt know
the verses of the whole cadre/ they determined to warn their com-
rade/ against this sorta man who cdnt recite poems/ & so her life as
a man with the men who were poets waz quite confusing & very
hassled.

so one day she decided that it waz probably awright that the men
who were poets thot of her as one of their own kind/ sometimes/ &
sometimes she waz mistaken for their mother/ or a misplaced lover/
but one day when she waz reading to the group/ in a pub some-
where in new york or california/ she said/ as a woman & a poet/
i've decided to wear my ovaries on my sleeve/ raise my poems on
my milk/ & count my days by the flow of my mensis/ the men who
were poets were aghast/ they fled the scene in fear of becoming un-
clean/ they all knew those verses/ & she waz left with an arena of
her own/ where words & notions/ imply 'she'/ where havin lovers is
quite common regardless of sex/ or profession/ where music &
mensis/ are considered very personal/ & language a tool for explor-
ing space/

the moral of the story:

#1: when words & manners leave you no space for yrself/ make a
poem/ very personal/ very clear/ & yr obstructions will join you or
disappear/

#2: if yr obstructions dont disappear/ repeat over & over again/ the
new definitions/ til the ol ones have no more fight in them/ then
cover them with syllables you've gathered from other dyin species/

#3: a few soft words have sent many a woman to her back with her
thighs flung open & eager/ a few more/ will find us standin up &
speakin in our own tongue to whomever we goddam please.

Barne's Landing/ February, 1977

i talk to myself

i can't quite remember how many questions or journalists or people
have happened to me in the last year. i can't even remember every-
thing i've said. i know i tried to convey my perceptions of the world,
of men & women, music & language, as clearly as i cd, but poets who
talk too much can trip over their own syllables. can become absurd.
like the time i told this woman that the most important thing that
ever happened to me waz my tail-cutting party. or the time i started
crying in the middle of a question cuz the person waz so nasty to me
i cd no longer speak. he said i had no right to exist/ so i said/ go
speak to a rightfully existing person, a white man, maybe. that's not
good press.

so the next time an interviewer said all he wanted waz for me to say
something controversial abt blk men. i said i love them. that waz no
press at all. so here i have a chance to talk to myself (which i really
do). all the time i'm asking myself. what the hell is going on with
you. i'll share this now with you. a conversation with all my selves.

tz: *how has all this hoopla & financial success changed yr life?*
i got to go to paris without marrying a rich man. i went to rio de jan-
eiro too.

tz: *i don't mean that, i mean, how has yr relationship with the world
changed?*
i have more control over what will happen to me. i like that. i don't
like that people think i knew from some unknown source that my
life waz gonna change. that somehow i cheapened myself by allow-
ing my piece to go to broadway. i don't like that people think i shd
be different from who i waz. i don't like that some people liked me

better when i waz powerless & worried all the time & now that i'm
not i have no more good qualities. you know how some people are
attracted to pitifulness. i'm not.

tz: *what exactly are you doing with yrself these days?*
i'm writing poems.

tz: *anything else?*
i'm still trying not to hate every minute i stay in new york. i am
working on a poemplay, *a photograph: a still life with shadows/ a
photograph: a study of cruelty.* & then there is the movie script i'm
trying to rewrite for *sassafrass.* & the work i do with *negress*, a third
world women's performing collective. then too, i have started to
work with david murray in a duo that is attempting to erase the
boundaries that cause the failure of most poems done with/ to
music. david & i are exploring the possibilities of integrating the me-
dium, so that the saxophone is not saying again what i just said/ nor
am i repeating what i just heard him do.

tz: *why did you always want to be an ikette?*
there waz a time in my life when rhythm & blues waz my only real-
ity. from the time i waz eight until i waz about thirteen years old i
wd sit by the radio in st. louis & listen to george logan's show, till my
mother insisted i had enuf of that niggah music. saturdays were
spent at vashon high school or at sumner high school (all colored)
watching jackie wilson tear his clothes off, dancing in the aisles to
ben e. king, the olympics, the shirelles. the only black folks with a
public aura were on the stage. now i cd never really sing, but i've al-
ways been able to "shake that thing." ike & tina turner were big big

big in st. louis. the ikettes got ta wear lil slinky skirts & be on the
stage where smokey robinson wd bend over & whisper abt "bad
girls." "she's not a bad girl because she wants to be free/ uhmmm,
she wants to be free." that waz what i wanted/ to be free to dance &
smile at the people having such a good time listening to tina turner
talk abt "i'm justa fool/ you know i'm in love." i imagine her songs
were for me what edna st. vincent millay's sonnets were for a terri-
bly romantic lil white girl thirty years ago.

tz: but how did you get from tina turner & the chantelles to bebop &
poetry?
my mother & father went to europe, cuba, haiti, and mexico. they
kept their friends around me from nigeria, togo, haiti, cuba, india,
the philippines, france & mexico. i heard so many languages, so
many different kinds of music. visits from dizzy gillespie, chico ham-
ilton, sonny til & chuck berry. i played a solo violin concert in the
fifth grade. i cdnt tell the difference tween notes & letters. an "a"
waz an "a" like a "b" waz another way of saying something. "i live
in language/ sound falls round me like rain on other folks." we
usedta have sunday afternoon family variety shows. my mama wd
read from dunbar, shakespeare, countee cullen, t.s. eliot. my dad wd
play congas & do magic tricks. my two sisters & my brother & i wd
do a soft-shoe & then pick up the instruments for a quartet of some
sort: a violin, a cello, flute & saxophone. we all read constantly. any-
thing. anywhere. we also tore the prints outta art books to carry
around with us. sounds/ images, any explorations of personal visions
waz the focus of my world. st. louis waz just desegregating herself,
while i grew. sometimes a langston hughes poem or a bobby tim-
mons tune waz the only safe place i cd find.

tz: *that might explain yr lifestyle. why you move so much & rarely keep a house more than a year.*

yes, it might. my parents were so mobile during my early childhood. i waz accustomed to traveling, since we moved so many times: from trenton, to upstate new york, to alabama, back to trenton, to st. louis & again back to trenton, before i waz thirteen. i never expected to have anywhere in particular to call home. the spaces i occupied in los angeles, boston, san francisco, & new york from 1969 till now have congealed, to the extent that i relate to those seventeen flats as one. they all look the same. the hangings i wove. the photos of the same friends. the same records. the same pots & pans. i surround myself with essentially the same people wherever i go.

we usedta call ourselves the COSMIC-DU-WOP COMMUNE. poets mostly & some musicians. thulani, jessica hagedorn, nashirantosha & pepo priester, pedro pietri, papoleto melendez, etnairis rivera, gylan kain, & carol le sanchez, & paul vane, roberto vargas, alejandro mur- guia, victor hernandez-cruz & tom cusan. we are all so transient. nothing changes too much for any of us. we write poems. we read the poems. we find out who pays money to read the poems. we go there. we read to each other, drink wine, walk the streets with each other making poems. we like to fall in love & be poets. i'm not sure anybody enjoys our stuff as much as we do. or even if people realize how essential poems are to our existence.

tz: *you mentioned a number of male writers. how do you account for yr reputation as a feminist, if you listen to & get nourishment from all these men?*

(*i laugh.*) some men are poets. they find wonderment & joy in them- selves & give it to me. i snatch it up quick & gloat. some men are poets. they fall prey to despair & ruin. when i feel sad, i go off with them/ carrying my sorrow on a leash. some men are poets & then, some men are just men who simply are not worth the time it takes to forget a bad idea. i stay far from them: i hear there is an epidemic of vacuity whenever they open their mouths.

tz: *wd you be willing to mention names?*
no.

tz: *well. how do you explain loving some men who write & some men who play music & some men who are simply lovable, when yr work for almost three years has been entirely woman-centered?*
i can do a lot of things. we all can. women haveta. i waz not able to establish the kind of environment i thot my work needed when i read with men all the time. you haveta remember there's an enormous ignorance abt women's realities in our society. we ourselves suffer from a frightening lack of clarity abt who we are. my work attempts to ferret out what i know & touch in a woman's body. if i really am committed to pulling the so-called personal outta the realm of non-art. that's why i have dreams & recipes, great descriptions of kitchens & handiwork in *sassafrass, cypress & indigo.* that's why in *for colored girls* . . . i discuss the simple reality of going home at nite, of washing one's body, looking out the window with a woman's eyes. we must learn our common symbols, preen them and share them with the world. the readings i usedta do with david henderson, conyus, bob chrisman, paul vane, tom cusan, roberto vargas & all the others at the coffee gallery, the intersection, & s.f. state were quite high. but the readings at the women's studies center, with the third world women's collective, international women's day affairs, with

the shameless hussy poets, these were overwhelmingly intense &
growing experiences for me as a woman & as a poet.

the collective recognition of certain realities that are female can still
be hampered, diverted, diluted by a masculine presence. yes. i segre-
gated my work & took it to women. much like i wd take fresh water
to people stranded in the mojave desert. i wdnt take a camera crew
to observe me. i wdnt ask the people who had never known thirst to
come watch the thirsty people drink.

i believe my work waz nourished & shaped to a large degree by the
time i spent with women. in san francisco i waz isolated in this very
close community of creative women. rosalie alphonso, elvia marta,
paula moss, halifu, ifa iyaun, laurie carlos, mari, wopo holup, j.j. wil-
son: all these women had something to do with *for colored girls* at
one stage or another/ have given me courage & insight. no one thinks
men relating as artistic collaborators is weird. we assume artists
need the energy of other artists. look at the music of the art ensem-
ble of chicago, air, or the world saxophone quartet, the chi-lites.
that's all cool/ they are all men. but women artists exploring what
we are in the world is still considered "breaking away" from normal.
groups like isis, gangbang, sagaris, the women's film festival, daugh-
ters inc. aren't included in normal. but we need ourselves to take
care of ourselves. it's as simple as that.

*tz: some white people think lorraine hansberry influenced you; since
she didn't, who did help you understand yr craft?*
around 1966/ abt the time i went to barnard i thot leroi jones (imamu
baraka) waz my primary jumping-off point. that i cd learn from him
how to make language sing & penetrate one's soul, like in *the dead
lecturer, the system of dante's hell,* & *black magic poetry.* then i

found myself relating technically to ishmael reed, particularly in terms of diction & myth, as in *yellow back radio broke-down* & *mumbo jumbo.* then i discovered the nostalgia david henderson can make so tangible; our immediate past as myth. & here comes pedro pietri, allowing language to create a world that can't exist outside his poems. i find victor hernandez cruz shows me how to say anything i thot i saw.

jessica hagedorn on the other hand puts the worlds we both share in a terribly personal & cosmopolitan realm. her book, *dangerous music,* says to me that complicated notions can be explicated by rhythm. we can approach difficult concepts with ourselves; there is no need to go the route of iowa to get a sophisticated poem. all the years i've been writing i've spoken constantly with thulani, whose poetry sustains me as much as my own. thulani teaches me to take risks. her familiarity with the new black music & her understanding of a woman's relationship to the universe continually push me to refuse to be afraid of what i am feeling.

then there is clarence major who has let fantasy loose for me. let me see language with no more responsibility than to give me an image/ however contorted, private & bizarre. clarence's stuff, like his novel *reflex & bone structure,* is breaking the linear tradition in black literature, moving us from narrative to the crux of the moment.

i've learned so much from latin americans too: julio cortazar, manuel puig, octavio paz, mario vargas llosa, miguel angel asturias, réné dépestre, gabriel garcía márquez, jacques roumain, léon damas. i get a western hemispheric reference that saves me from what is insidious in north american & european literature/ the suggestion that black people exist only as vehicles for white people's fantasies. the technical skill & brilliance of the characterizations of garcía márquez

have raised my expectations of how well a reader shd know a person/ place.
& then there is neruda . . .

tz: *i thot you said all art forms contributed to yr development?*
i didn't say it yet. i thot abt saying that what dianne mcintyre's sounds-in-motion dance company does with cecil taylor's music gives me the right to put the axis of a poem off balance & hold. i wanted to say i learn abt lyricism from david murray's saxophone & romare bearden's collages. i wanted to insist i've learned abt beauty from carmen delavallade's dancing & albert ayler's music.

tz: *yes, but what do you believe a poem shd do?*
quite simply a poem shd fill you up with something/ cd make you swoon, stop in yr tracks, change yr mind, or make it up. a poem shd happen to you like cold water or a kiss.

tz: *one more thing. what is it like to be you?*
good. good. sometimes more trouble than i like to handle cuz i didn't take care of myself the way i cd have had i known i waz worth loving. but then i have a bunch of raucous memories i have survived to giggle abt/ that has to be awright. i am becoming less afraid of who this "zaki" is.

Ms. Magazine/ December 1977

love & other highways

oh let my love come tumbling in
into our lives again
saying
oh baby i love you
& i want you to know right now
i want to give you some love
some good good loving.

—bob marley & the wailers

its happenin/ but you dont know abt it

(for david)

these kisses are clandestine
no one can see them
i hold them in my hand
shd i be discovered/
i stick them in my hair & my head gets hot
so i haveta excuse myself

under no circumstances
can the legs that slip over my hips
leave tellin marks/ scents
of love/ this wd be unpardonable
so i am all the time
rubbin my arms/ exposin myself
to river mists/ to mask the sweetness
you leave me swillin in

i cant allow you to look at me
how you do so i am naked & wantin
to be explored like a honeysuckle patch
when you look at me how you do so
i am all lips & thigh/
my cover is blown & the kisses
run free/ only to hover sulkin over
yr cheek/ while i pretend
they are not mine
cuz its happenin/ but you dont know abt it

the kisses they take a slow blues walk
back to me

in the palm of my hand
they spread out/ scratch kick curse & punch
til my skin cries/
kisses raisin hell/ in my fists/
they fly out mad & eager
they'll fly out mad & eager
if you look at me how you do so i am naked
& wantin/ if you look at me how you do so
i am all lips & thigh/
they gonna fly out mad & eager
they fly out & climb on you
the kisses/ they
flyin
if you look at me
how you do so

where the mississippi meets the amazon

(for david murray)

you fill me up so much
when you touch me
i cant stay here
i haveta go to my space

people talk to me
try to sell me cocaine
play me a tune
somebody wanted to give me a massage
but i waz thinkin abt you
so i waz in my space

i'm so into it
i cant even take you

tho i ran there with you
tho you appear to me by the riverbed

i cant take you
it's my space
a land lovin you gives me

shall i tell you how my country looks
my soil & rains
there's a point where the amazon meets the mississippi
a bodega squats on the eiffel tower
toward mont saint michel

i'm so into it
i cant even take you

it's my space
a land lovin you gives me

there's a bistro there near the pacific
& the pyramid of the moon is under my bed
i can see the ferry from trois islets to rio
from my window/ yr eyes caress my shoulders

my space is a realm of monuments & water
language & the ambiance of senegalese cafes

i cant take you tho
you send me packin/ for anywhere/ i've never known
where we never not exist
in my country we are/ always
you know how you kiss me
just like that

where the nile flows into the ganges
how the arc de triomphe is next to penn station
where stevie wonder sleeps in a d# whole note
& albert ayler is not in the east river

my space
where i sip chablis from yr mouth
& grow roses in my womb

where the mississippi meets the amazon
neruda still tangoes in santiago at dawn
where i live

jean-jacques dessalines is continually re-elected
the moon sometimes scarlet

i cant take you
but i'll tell you
all i can remember
when you touch me

lovin you is ecstasy to me

25 years w/ the art ensemble
mad preachers & painted banjo half-moons smilin from
brown cheeks blowin chicago city fires in the western bay/
my plan dream n occasion of occasions/ to decorate my ¼ century
self w/ joseph's rhythms n roscoe's visions never transpired
cuz
de white man say/ $6000 too much for niggahs to play a fuckin horn

i entered the new saga in a volvo satiated with peach incense &
the shirelles cryin
        'mama said there'd be days like this
        there'd be days like this my mama said
'hey hey hey/ the bay bridge becomes dorothy's tornado in kansas &
i fly to a new oz/ moreno y dulce/ tho my gold shoes are layin up
w/ de pinoy princess of the avenues/ the ocean ringin her neck
like the tufts of macaws in frangipangi trees/
i am speedy/   miss speedo to you in the cosmic du-wah/
        dom dom dom dom dom dom de du de
        dom dom dom dom dom whaaaaaaaaaa dom de du deeee
yeah yeah yeah
yeaaaaaaaaaa
i saida hey lil girl come n go wit me
this is the rainbow, my dear
to be tap danced over in our razmatazzz regalia/
blkbirds 1924/ i'll bring the sequins, you bring de flou-nce
n all my lives of every year can pass
sassy n free from me to you/

i thought i saw a flock of flamingoes meditatin
cross dere from de bekin's furniture warehouse/

bt i waz mistaken/
peacocks have sequestered themselves by the docks
singin dirges
n rufflin feathers ego had too abundantly supplied/
i hold everybody's hand/
some people's bodies are sweat next to me/
mquanda mweli tarabu mikey mr. nim/
m'sieur henri
serenades the honkytonk women in nashira's kitchen/
baratted barbara serves lily flowers pickled ginger
blk tree fungus   & spiced broth in aluminum plates/
ifa is manifest in furtive greens
& the blueness of her eyes floats
round my heart/
wines of blkberry apricot organic apples
bounce in my heart/
the empress singes opium over de stove/
joints seem taped to taxi's index finger/
norman   didn't bring his drums/
kapuenda is embroidered with cornelians
njeri is lavender/

surprise surprise happy birthday to you
happy birthday to you/
happy birthday nashira n zake/
HAPPY HAPPY BIRTHDAY BABY!!!
tho you've found somebody new/
sheoli leans on the kitchen sink/
she is radiant & strawberry almond bread

tastes of her love/
ms. jazz-a-belle glistens over boilin pots
she is pineapples bananas melons peaches
sour cream n honey/
she is the other half of the turquoise moon/
victor struts w/ rolled shoulders
carryin ancient toltecas in his forearms/
the bells keep on ringin/
baby washington reminds me/
the dues i've paid/
corners of arms & dinky hotels
forgotten with mushrooms n pills/
lovers absolved
my conspiracy to get out from carin/
like the marvellettes never sang a song
that wazn't mine/
& de postman's looking for news of you/
twistin shingalin down de street/

any day now/
chuck jackson's screamin/
love will let me down/
cuz you won't be arounnnd/
the bells become the tingle of new days
love is ever slippin out tho
halifu's freckles won't go away/
tomasin can only make me love her more/
nana places the chalice of dream in my hands/
greg leaves a flower on my door/

women brown n bangled almost-not-here/
slow samba down lombard street
all around me/

bakayoko he loved the harlot
who cd tear herself
to protect the mad begger/
bakayoko loved the harlot
& she died alone in the struggle/
but i aint gonna die off/
widout lovin every nook & cranny
where don't nobody go alone/
i gotcha in me/
& *lovin you is ecstasy to me/*
wont ever leave you/
nononononononoooooooooo
lovin you is ecstasy to me

'this woman thinks we're de beauvoir & jean-paul/
never forget/ i'ma spic & yr a colored girl'

shd i have said like the lady & ben w.
or wd jus mentionin 'my man he'll never know . . .'
this is not paris/ not even the yucatan
i cant get away wita allusion to a god/ & his woman
who waz rain/
this is true yr a spic & i'ma colored girl
how much more unlikely cd two lovers be/

really
look at the women on the corner
in any day/ accosted by a righteous drunkard
or they husbands/
see a child/ 12 & tough in hips & much too much smile
for a impossibility/ look at the lovers we know
shd i wanna be a bessie in yr winter
a begger in yr dream/ a night masqueradin for yr mama
i may not be the spirit woman of the forest/
may never know a kingdom of ritual & gold-spun cloth
i'll never hold a gun to yr head to 'click' & let me laugh
i'll never stand on the wood bridge round from my ol
house screamin 'you a goddammed muthafuckah' witta bottle
in my hand broken & red/

& i dont expect to be left in the loneliest
of beds/ wit mamie & bessie to comfort me/ in
a kitchen of solo boleros preparin dinner for some
mouth that walks & shuts doors behind him

look
really
whatta unlikely wonder is we/
lovers in a seaport kinda way/ like garbo in the fog
& cinqúe in refute/ this is how i hold yr head
where bombas jump all up/ in & outta ayler/ &
lil painted lips/ léon damas & ornette cd getta hold of me
when we talk/ i am swept up like janie that first
night/ teacake hadda yen so southern/ so you/ know
this is unprecedented/ dont pay no mind
to ol models/ ol tunes make me grin
like big maybelle & freddie washington's voices/
they legs so brown/ strong/ any woman shd be/ so here
for you/ the way we wrap up in the mornin/ is
all our world
we're entitled

several propositions in the middle of the nite
when i am travellin between virginia & nyc &
i dont know where you are but i'm working on it

you are as sweet as magnolia milk
in dark spanish coffee
si negro yo soy bustelo

how abt a trip to rio
how abt lobster/ artichoke hearts dipped in brandy
how abt a watermelon batidos
how wd you like it?

tu ris. je suis contente.
je ne veux pas beaucoup maintenant
seulement ta bouche prés de mes jambes
ou d'autresparts, que penses-tu?

it's COSMIC   it's ASTRAL
    WHIRLY-TWIRLY
        CELESTIAL
                        will it fit in here

you can call me clover &
roll in it all over & over
& over & over & over . . .

si tu me quieres
dime que si

je suis ici
pour toi
jusqu'il y a une lune rouge
chante entre mes doits
me faz feliz

37/

lotsa body & cultural heritage/

can i have a word   the word wid you
like the spinners waz talkin bout a
            MIGHTY LOVE
        MIGHTY MIGHTY MIGHTY MIGHTY LOVE
that grabs me
   i'm thinkin black & realizin
colored
cant stand no man to be callin me *BABEE*
to my face/
   but if i hear some stylistics du-wah/
donchu know i wanna give it away
BABEEEEEEEEE YOU MAKE ME FEEL SO BRAND NEW
feel brand new
& there's another strut i cant do widout
satiné suits & lamé cuffs
   volcano blue crepe shirts & heavy chests
like muhammad ali gone & learned
        to charm a lady
            sweep a child to womanhood from the stage
                make mama scream
                    & she don't know that man's name
UE-WAH-UE-WAH-EU-WAH-OW-HAAAAAAAaaaaa
the audacity of the blues

        rock me daddy
      roll me   daddy
      rock n roll me at the bijou   de uptown
      in soldan's gym
         saw jackie

        tear his shirt
throw it to us
        smokey leanin over de lights
sighin for us
                    &
        OH-OH-OOOOOOOO—BABY—BABYYYYYYYY
LET ME BUILD YOU A CASTLE
                bring all the hornplayers i know/
gonna sing & shout like the babysitters
trying to entertain
me/
        do the chicken   do the slop
chantels gonna chiffon & pearl applique
theyselves all over dis room
                & MAYBE MAYBE
                IF I PRAY EVERY NITE
                YOU'LL COME BACK TO ME

& i'ma rock
& i'ma roll
in all of them free music blues
joseph bowie
        knows what
i'm talkin bout   the art ensemble
jumped the r & b train headin for saturn
on saturday nite is colored

                i aint lyin
them flyin capes

exaggerated broken hearts teasin me
when the drifters go down them
railroad tracks
    THERE SHE GOES
        THERE GOES MY BABY
            MOVIN ON DOWN THE LINE
archie shepp & frank lowe
    whatchu blowin bout
        THERE SHE GOES
            THERE SHE GOES
& it's a blk & blue holiday
    in atlantic city
        club harlem
bein colored on the 4th of july

I'MA LOOKIN
I'M LOOKIN
I'M LOOKIN   *OH LOOKIN FOR A LOVE*
        TO CALL MY OWN

i aint particular
what kinda guitar
you got
    long as
you can play
me/ that song
    daddy
        rock me daddy
        roll me daddy

bring me them
rhythms & blues
i'ma neo-afrikan lady   but
    I GOTTA GOTTA GOTTA GOTTAGOTTA GOTTAGOTTA
get me some of rock & rollsssssssss

c'on albert
    where you at
c'on albert
    where are you at
i'ma ride yr ribald squeal
like
chuck berry   roosters in st-louis

sun-ra & horace
bring all the heliotropical folks
to this heah
    ROCK N ROLL REVIEW
bring me some ol roots
irresistible
    BA DA DADA DADA DA DA DA ADA DUMMMMMMMM

listen cecil mcbee/ listen heah ike turner
got me all gainst the wall & i waznt goin nowhere
nowhere but
home
nowhere but home
you bettah tell somebody to meet me
tell somebody to meet me

41/

       & tell me something good
tell me that you love me   *YEAH YEAAHHHHHHH*
bring a lil
delfonics in yr smile/
march clifford thornton all thru heah

rock me daddy
roll me daddy
deliver yrself
     SO FINE SOOOOOOO FINE YEAH SO FINE
     MY BABY SO DOGGONE FINE
& free/
    & sing it to me
SING   it to me

i'ma neo-afrikan lady but
    i GOTTAGOTTAGOTTA GOTTA GOTTA GOTTA
have me some of that rock n roll
for de new land

hands & holding

1)
hands & holding
tongues & clits
go well together
the way
the sun kisses the ocean at dawn
you have fallen
from the inside
of laughin congas
i hear you smilin
in the tunnel
women glissade
from tree limbs
their hips are so glad
to see you

2)
in the night/ ochun's candles
make ether-glow waves
thru the hairs on yr stomach
i have spoken to stars
confined to black holes
from the milky way
they want to fall round you
i am envied by ladies
brighter even than the sun

3)
you were curled
under the window
like kittens at mykko's tits
some visitors
took you towards the true rainbow
you slept
eyes wide water soft
i sat at the end of the rainbow
makin gumbo in a pot of gold

4)
a trinidadian woman
tells me a hot-blooded man
dances like slow winds
in haitian hills/
yr touch is firm
like roots to soil

5)
i cannot speak
yr eyes have
stolen my tongue
only knows
to move from yr lips
to yr thigh

& then

(for jules)

is it possible to come
with you and be away from
you/ simultaneously
can i love you and not hold you/
do it seem whatever may/ then also shall
if it's s'posed/ or
is the dragonfly correct in his
assertion that fools are those
who think and believe
then act like they knew
somethin abt livin while death
was inappropriately invited out
to lunch by cajolin rationalizations
wearing star-spangled elekes and
wooing ochun's last/ and fastest
daughter/ maybe not in sight
but in the visions of eyes
larger than our palms
there's a carnival of winged moons
and caring/ and i've
gotta love you and not have you as
a glass covered marble in my
back pocket/ i've gotta love you and
not know you as belonging to an ever
sides glistenin songs rockin
small trees in mossy cradles &
valleys burstin with green lakes in
shade flowers are the only/ binding

and freeness with you one answer
to being and loving with you
an october breeze

night letter #3

the telephone company is harassin me in my
sleep   everybody keeps callin
'hello hello'   old lovers i never want to see
lovers i'm dyin to meet   'hello hello'
i dont know who to answer
i say who is this/   so i'll know how to talk
to em/   what do you want   i'm sleepin
& everythin you say is a lie/   i'm makin you
up to call in my sleep cuz there are so many
disconnections in the day

say there operator   i need some assistance
i move my hand from my ear   (there is no telephone
in my bed   i am sweaty from the cat's fur
on my face)   there is no one to nestle
in the middle of my dreams
to hold me
everybody goes to a phone in my sleep
to call me up
they love me so much

      DING DONG   DING DONG   DING DONG
the special ring of my dream telephone waz $6.31 a month
more than regular service for unlimited local calls

you didnt call at noon
but at dawn in my dream you ring & laugh
cuz all i can make up for you to say is
'do you love me'

conversations with self disguised as you i wd have close
so i wake in the cold oakland fog
my eyes stingin with tears
in the telephone conversation it waz
almost you
you almost admitted not bein able
to leave me alone/ almost said
you wd come across the bridge to see me
(& my face is swollen/ red on the right side
where i lean on the metallic telephone wires)
i dont believe you will refuse to keep the engagements
we made inside my sleep
                        thulani is comin for lunch
                jessica is goin to speak to auntie pearl bout my sequins
        conyus is bakin mandarin chickens
& nashira is holdin a plant for me
today i'm gonna go see my friends
who called me up last night in my sleep

it is so   it is real
i cd not hear yr voices so perfect
if yr spirits werent runnin in the
night air/ in my telephone nightgown i stood on the porch
waitin for the one of you sposed
to take me to breakfast
                it is so   it is real
gene quoted a swami in boston
                'visions are messages of those who love us'
& i know you love me cuz everybody

called at the same time
you all called to let me know what you were doin
but when i woke   exhausted from
chattin all night   i go to meet you
& where are you   callin somebody
who can talk in the daytime

this is destroyin my writin
my dancin suffers from continual interruption
operators makin yr collect calls everywhere i go
'hello hello do you love me   hello hello hello stop ringin me up
if you cant remember dreams/ i cant be yr friend
if you dont
keep
the
appointment

you direct yr spirit to make connections/
leave me on the wharf
callin sea gulls

get it & feel good

you cd just take what
he's got for you
i mean what's available
cd add up in the long run
if it's music/ take it
say he's got good
dishwashing techniques
he cd be a marvelous
masseur/ take it
whatever good there is to
get/ get it & feel good

say there's an electrical
wiring fanatic/ he cd
come in handy some day
suppose they know how to tend plants
if you want somebody
with guts/ you cd go to a rodeo
a prize fight/ or a gang war might be up your alley
there's somebody out there
with something you want/
not alla it/ but a lil
bit from here & there can
add up in the long run

whatever good there is to get
get it & feel good
this one's got kisses
that one can lay

linoleum
this one likes wine
that one fries butter fish
real good
this one is a anarcho-musicologist
this one wants pushkin to rise again
& that one has had it with the past tense/
whatever good there is to get/
get it & feel good
this one cd make music
roll around the small of
yr back & that one jumps
up & down in the gardens
it cd be yrs
there really is enuf to get
by with in this world but
you have to know what yr looking
for/ whatever good there is to get
get it & feel good
you have to know what
they will give up easily
what's available is not always
all that's possible
but there's so much fluctuation
in the market these days
you have to be
particular
whatever good there is to get
get it & feel good

whatever good there is to get
get it & feel good/ get it & feel good
snatch it & feel good
grab it & feel good
steal it & feel good
borrow it & feel good
reach it & feel good
you cd
   oh yeah
     & feel good.

closets

Listen more to things
Than to words that are said
The water's voice sings
And the flame cries.
And the wind that brings
The woods to sigh
Is the breathing of the dead.

—Birago Diop

senses of heritage

my grandpa waz a doughboy from carolina
the other a garveyite from lakewood
i got talked to abt the race & achievement
bout color & propriety/
nobody spoke to me about the moon

daddy talked abt music & mama bout christians
my sisters/ we
always talked & talked
there waz never quiet
trees were status symbols

i've taken to fog/
the moon still surprisin me

just as the del vikings stole my heart

    (oh auntie emma)

my fairy godmother retired
with the brown vs. ferguson decision
she reasoned i waz divested of my separate
but equal status & waz entitled
to whatever lil white girls got
from whoever they got it from
since she waz raised in greener pastures
& knew the devil only in the blues saw-dust
of a raunchy dawn/ a cruel dance on the edge of a dime
so she retired/
she waznt bout to misegenate her powers/
integrate em either/
leavin me to fend for myself

i've felt her absence from the moment she escaped
with my love of who i am/ conjurin myself
thru catcalls & mailbox cherry bombs was not my forte
i learned only by breakin the law/
                    i am separate
                    i am equal
i live my own lil rock/
cover my own back anywhere i wanna go
& i go anywhere i want
crackers are born with the right to be alive
i am making mine up
right here in your face
             why dont you
                  go on
& push me

    55/

inquiry

my questions concern the subject poetry
is whatever runs out/ whatever digs my guts
til there's no space in myself
cryin wont help/ callin mama wont help
lovers are detours/ no way to assuage this
poem/ but in the words & they are deceitful/
images beat me confuse me/ make me want all of you to share me/
& i hide under my bed/

poetry is unavoidable connection/
some people get married/ others join the Church
i carry notebooks/ so i can tell us what happened/
midnight snacks in bed with whoever/ are no compensation/ when
i'm listenin to multitudes of voices/ i consume yr every word &
move/

durin the day you are initiated into *the holy order*
of prospective poems/ i dream in yr voice/ sometimes act
yr fantasies/ i've made them my own/
whatever is here/ is what you've given me/
if it's not enough for you/
give me some more

i'm not very communicative

i'm not very communicative
gettin my poems to you
isnt easy for me
i dance most times
when i'm lonely i
pull pearl beads cross
my window-scape/ i ride
the freeway/ trolley lines
climb trees/ i walk
i hear young
girls cursin
their mothers & old
men coughin
to rid themselves of phlegm
always makin em whisper
i avoid friends
i dance
i make grits to ease
pre-menstrual obsessions
a desperate fear of laziness
hurtin someone &
not reachin you

i had five nose rings

i had five nose rings
                a gold circle
                a silver circle
                a star
                nefertiti
                & a half moon
without these i am unarmed
not ready for   arbitrary violence
paris winds in winter
                my face chafed/ seemingly rouged
                a positive response
                to poison
my decorations   emblems   fetishes
gleaming from my cheeks as the sun turns waters to diamond
these beauties of mine   crawled   poison
to the base of my brain
like cocaine is apt to do
vitamin deficiency
a lack
of fresh air & music

the ring on my face/ like a brand
or an emerald
paris snarls her fog & chill thru my veins
throws me to
the outskirts of myself

i had five nose rings
                a gold circle

                    a silver circle
                    a star
                    nefertiti
                    & a half moon
i am no longer suspected of being/ moslem
i am suspected of scarring myself
my one claim to shout abt
my era of myself
becomes a signal of depression

unadorned i march along these avenues
my head darting forward/ down
no one to see the mark
the absence of the jewel
my face betrays me

i frequent corners where men beat each other to death
                    in the name of
                    love

                    i know children who carry knives
                    to preserve the dignity of their innocence
                    guns to frighten anyone who comes
                    too close/ contact
is dangerous here
makes us susceptible to disease

the air in paris warped my visions/ gave
distance & psychosis clearance

59/

sometimes there is too much poison
to attend to beauty
i had five nose rings
        a gold circle
        a silver circle
        a star
        nefertiti
        & a half moon
they have fallen away

i breathe now
this lack of beauty
& caress the cheek of a child
who imagines no thing
beautiful
no thing
safe
paris   new york
linger in the blood
like malaria   scarlet fever   typhoid
herpes simplex   herpes complex   syphilis   gonorrhea
linger in the blood
like disease

frank albert & viola benzena owens

she waited on the 7th floor
corner flat   her children   wanderin
from room to room   ghosts   ghost children
effie   althea   rosalie
                    diptheria deserted
blonde colored girls   bright-migrant
children never runnin carolinian hills
never utterin   gullah accents
                    slurrin words like bajans
mountain folk

they wandered
rosalie   althea   effie   in white
lace dresses   starched for the wake
celebrated births on 52nd street   swallowed
like placenta   when there is nothin/ else
when you rear yr young in dark closets
like a stray cat
        she waited by the door
opened to aunties from his side of the family
uncles from charleston   a loyal bartender   &
children in bodies
                    only hintin of ochre soil
she lingered by the corrupted window
by the fire escape   soot-sprinkled plants
laughed at her   meticulous   ventures
washin
sills   diapers   the carpenter's trousers
her hair

                  languid in the nape of the neck
a thick wad of soft nap   above the mole
she wanted a 'bob'   a fashionable diversion
to save pushin thick braids off her chest
while she leaned

                        over steamin laundry
                        the baby
                        the father
                        & the graves
she waited for him at the kitchen
table heaped with buttered rice n okra
heaped with linen napkins from the allendale wedding
the children in bodies gorged themselves
on halves of biscuits   they prided
themselves for lovin him   the father
they waited   & she drew sketches
of her mother   who had died   her sisters
who had died   her father who had died
in jacksonville & left her to speak
too proper for a workman   too poor
for somethin better   the carpenter
was solid   was handsome   was kind &
delivered her north
delivered her too many to suckle
& still sass him   she waited/ her hair
so heavy   her head hung down
to fondle the baby
warm the baby
move the baby from colored manhattan

take the baby north to freedom
to the bronx   she waited for deliverance
for him to return
from tendin the fire
from passin for irish
from the bar where faster women rolled
from the garveyites sneering at pale
        niggahs all livin together
in special wings of tenements

she waited & mumbled
    'his eye is on the sparrow
    & i know he's watchin me/ he's watchin me'
she poured grease over turnip greens
asked the haitian roomer to move
for workin voodoo on the baby
dyin   from scarlet fever
warm the baby pray   save
the child
        he loved his own
        he loved his own

she sweat & brought breath to his blood
he lied in the world   he looked over his
shoulder   every step   to see
the burnin cross   feathers/ ruins of farms
his father's tools   she waited
by the bed
        fingerin his tuskegee photo

the carpenter's shop   the colored pioneers
the baby was purple/ foamin at the mouth
she waited   for christ
to reveal himself   she sang
                        compulsively
to soothe the baby
ease his entry
the door never opened
he lay in the cellar   fractured   crumbled
over   un-even casing   the carpenter
crawled without his body   thru sicilian ashes/
jewish cadavers moanin in the beams/
he crawled to his children
rosalie   althea   effie in lace dresses starched for the wake
roamin from room to room   swallowed like placenta
his   woman   waitin   receivin   the   spirits
carolina screams/ branded up country slaves/ raging

                he made the journey
                        to deliver her   to freedom
                                the carpenter   tendin   to his   own
                                        movin   north

the old men

the old men meet
round 2:00 maybe ten to
share nudges & loneliness

#1 opens his door always in dressin gown
& stockin cap/ he invites #2 in
they sit on the porch/ brown stiff
beer cans sit awkward in their fingers
thick knuckles like small ax-handles

#3 leans on the picket fence
there is no grass here/
small wine bottles/ #4 walks round the corner
his top left pocket frayin/ the old men
walk with
old pictures   secrets   wishes

the old men
sit on either side of the stoop
hands dangle between their legs
#1 tips the brim of his straw hat/ #3
stretches a lame leg
#4 chews his beer cud-like
sadness like the regularity of young women passin
#2 nods his head same as the bleached willow
#4 pulls his moustache into the corners
of his mouth/ they're from round here/
they meet everyday with old pictures   secrets   wishes

an ol fashion lady

she's got whiskers
bout quarter inch long 'n
a tattered grey sweater
hangin round mismatched
shoulders one reachin
toward the a&p sign
the other barely holdin on
her hat they's a pieced
together daisy 'n some
witherin blue velvet
like the evenin jacket
under the sweater wit
gold lamé appliqué
set off by these teensy
butterflies wit pink 'n
lavender wings flyin
over two/ three missin
buttons at her bosom
reachin a good 6 inches
towards this rope round her waist
she waz steppin lively now
on 8th avenue movin
awkward round comely
females feelin mangoes
sortin beans & lookin at
brassieres 'n girdles
she waz movin
her shrivelin head from side
to side   askin who

which one of us wd
go in wit her to the
beauty shop testifyin
that our old friend wdnt
say nothin that
she wd be still she wd pay
like anybody else
to get her hair fixed
somethin like lena
in stormy weather

in honor of yr poise in the face of hungry lions/
aquanetta/ carmen miranda/ florence mills/ & ms. dandridge

(for mary hope lee)

yr hips n sequin slippers
scamper in the nights

flowers grow thru 2nd story windows
time-step jasmine eyes into my shimmies
of childhood
wantin to know
how to make my
smile nourish
WWII g.i.'s/
            the way ya usedta/ in the movies
yr satin shoulders toyed with generals
& managers of flophouses pinched yr ass
dirt clingin to the bottoms
of yr shoes n the tassels on yr bosoms
never went the same direction/
                        bob hope n harry belafonte
                            followed you everywhere/
in yr mirrors
yr mothers frowned cuz you slept so many places/

the callin cards of 20th century-fox-pr-men
decorated the antique washtub in the hall
i have washed myself in trumpet arpeggios
maracas dangled from my waist
the way bananas glazed yr eyebrow
the courts abducted yr children
for singin one too many

i see darkness under yr eyes
petals of salt round yr mouth/
i knew even as a child
you always cried
before the dance

EXPIRIESE GIRL WANTED

1)

whatchu gonna do
wid all them
ho-mo-ny grits, gal
donchu know
up north
niggahs
don' eat no fried grits
we eat blueberry
pan . . . cakes
like at the pan cake house
there is some fools
think they african eatin rice & shit
but they dont bothah nobody
naw they don' mean a thing

2)

pass the salt, please there honey
i wanta put some salt
on these eggs 'n grits
hey girl
where's my check
cantchu move no fastern that
come up heah 'n forget how to act
if i waz a white man
sheeeeit   if i waz a white man
i betchu wd jump
cross that counter
wantin to gimme

some of that there
bushy pussy
huh, gal

3)
i seen ya wid that dude
BLAM BLAM   baaaang
                    OOOOOOOO oooooooh
i say i seen ya
tits pushed halfway down his throat
BLAM BLAM BLAM
                    OOOOOO oooo oh honey
i aint gonna tell ya again
BLAM BLAM
ya cant sell what aint yours 'n
BLAM BLAM
everything you got
BLAMMMMM BLAM bang bang BLAMMMMMMmmmm
                    HOOOOOOOOOOoooooooooooooh
everything you got/ girl/ is mine
BLAM BLAM   ya undastand
sit down 'n shut up

4)
i'm tellin ya
that niggah's got some nerve
bringin that bitch up heah   in my house
she aint nothin but a
big ol hole wit painted fingernails

i know she cant get him off
like i can/ i know just what to do wit that stuff
girl/ i know that man
'sides
aint nobody's cunt golden

    5)
yeah, mama
i like new york fine
yeah, mama
i gotta real nice job
uh huh, in a restaurant
real nice folks come there
uh huh i get good tips
everybody's been treatin me real nice
& i'ma send for you 'n daddy
soon as i get to know my way roun'
       'n get usedta
          usedta . . . . . .

telephones & other false gods

  (for pedro and musa)

i feel very unsafe
in the presence of
meat-eaters   those
who charge me interest
for allowin them entrance
to my dreams where
they insult holy visitors
from this realm & other
creatures i have encountered
durin my stay among you

the livin very often have no dime to make
local telephone calls & 911 is a figment of
muggers' imaginations while they bludgeon
faggots' eyes & rape women who have never
been loved or taken out to dinner

i'm gonna have
my phone turned off
every night that matancera's
trumpets take me to the underground
garden   so i can visit laughter's rhythms
        before she remembers
                        the A train
& comes cruelly after
subterranean passengers
who read eastern airlines
advertisements
without askin forgiveness

from women who can't find
fresh okra on tuesday evenin
who tried very hard to be
good bell telephone operators
but got fired cuz it was impossible
to locate human beings in the
new york city directory

while my phone is off the hook
i'm goin to see that nostrand avenue
has a candle burnin & a neon light
rally will be held for the right
to semi-annual garbage collections
& children who no longer reek
of surplus dried milk can play
in backyards without bein molested
by the policeman from staten island
who makes it in his wife's ass
when he gets a chance to kick
a niggah's balls he salivates &
dreams of raspberry toast'ems

meat-eaters disrupt the melody
causin great anguish among pregnant
ladies and cocoons can no longer
tolerate arbitrary judges at beauty
contests mispronouncin african bodies
for a trip to las vegas
& many many gin-scarred nights

with ideal union leaders
eatin grapes & lettuce while
their wives do 's&m' experiments
on house girls from trinidad
who only get 3 hours off
to clean their wounds on
tuesday night when there
is no fresh okra or dancin
allowed with heterosexual men

how can you keep dialin my number when
it's obvious i only answer those who need
no phone to call
        who can meander
                casually
thru intense yearnings
without askin
why
geechees carry razors &
mingle w/
only tropical souls

i will not
persist in allowin you to exploit me
makin my dreams into nightmares
of san francisco devils
w/ minstrel faces & opium
withdrawal blues will not be given
tickets to my circus where

everythin is free
but very expensive
for those who use
their names to pay
for the trouble of
supportin parasitic
ego/
horn players & poets
will be discouraged from
            lyin
            prostrate
            before
            wax images &
women
        will once again learn
                to be like
                        the wind

            there are no intermissions
when the record is over celia cruz
& i will sing for those acquainted
with 50¢ flowers
                central park on weekdays
        will be available for lovin old trees
& rememberin
to speak highly
            of fats waller
            who cd have
                saved us

rememberin
rememberin   to speak
              highly
                 of
                     fats
                        waller

      who cd have
      saved
      us
      from self-imposed
      busy signals & the stench
      of vampires loose on the streets
      sufferin with gout & tape-recorded
      reaction to small children in
      fallen wagons
old women
wrapped in paper bags
continue to dream of
porcelin teeth & a place
to wash
cuz in their dreams
they can hold babies & visit their daughters
w/ out looking for a dime to call
findin all the circuits
took a vacation & the computer
has no listin for displaced
africans usin aliases
to escape the cries of spirits
callin managin to

visit durin nights
of typhoons hurricanes blackouts
&
other
festive
occasions
that
bring
families
together
natural disasters prohibit lovers from exchangin phone #s
make us stay by someone
to forget
to answer   doorbells
ringin telephones   suspend   us
in the melodrama of tv serials
& women who dont cook fresh
vegetables or remind their
men of orange blossoms & sultry conga drums
comin to un-do what's been done
comin to un-do what's been done
comin to un-do what's been done
hurricanes   floods   earthquakes   & blackouts
natural disasters make us stay by someone
stay by someone .
festive occasions
stay here

odessa

carries an old sweater
a woolworth bobbie-soxer wig
sits right on top her head
her eyes are quick & puffed
one scar under her chin
with bedroom slippers
she sits on her porch
her grandchildren try
to play when she isn't shoutin
'bring me a cold beer, heah'
odessa
came over
to invite me to coffee
she reached my door
wondered did i keep
any johnny walker blk/

who am i thinkin of

(for beverly)

when i write   i think of my friends
the people of my visions
but how cd i presume to think of men
who leave so little behind   i find them
in my wash cloth   in the dirty dishes
by my unmade bed
when i write i erase these dark halls
lone subway stops   the car followin
too closely   how cd i presume
to address my self
to men
they leave so little behind
& still i dont remember.

once a poet
delivered valentino
on a tie-dyed sheet w/
tequila passion
the sheik gallopin a desert for me
another sketched me
in the midst of bougainvillea
another saturated my basement with painted skeletons
long ago a poet
telephoned from ny
to have breakfast
in seattle

i've waded in hidden creeks
with the men i remember
the others had no sense of humor

80/

latin night is monday

(for alejandro at the ribeltad)

monday night is latin night
every night some other slot
on monday mambo
tuesday good-foot
wednesday belly-slither
thursday sleep
friday catch riffs
saturday make yr own music

monday night is latin night
i wanna bomba wednesday
are you gonna arrest me
for gettin my rhythms confused
i cd good-foot thursday
to make up for missin the beat

monday night is latin night
but trumpets & congas are my blood
i shd seek out a coffin
fly outta hydrant/ monday
night is latin night
they are very strict/ how we live
is important business/ latin night only monday
is contagious/ dangerous
let us be ourselves/ every day

fame on all fours

1)
i wrote in san francisco on
a 4 by 12 board
plywood unfinished
covered with pink & yellow squares
i knew 3 people
    one friend in baltimore
    a friend with child
    one friend in love
i wrote feedin my selves
with no tongue
    no mouth
that we might understand/
                "what's happenin here?"
yng men in vintage vw's honk horns
crackers from texas apologize
poets hallucinate all feet in water chilled & pure
high as dancers leap beyond gravity in the tenderloin
a student hangs a 16 ft. swing by my door
i hold the waist of a veteran on a harley-davidson
in the rain/ he wants to drink poetry
settles for coors

2)
fame gets on the typewriter in new york/
          "the magenta ribbon wont do
          nor orange nor aqua
          have you no black ribbon
            have you nothin ordinary
          i've never imagined 3 lovers in a day

told a critic he suffers from malignancy
bitch/ who are you talking to
i work every day/ my kids are illiterate
they dont even cherish clarabelle
i've a maidenform everything/ niggahs
have no tactile sense of cotton any more
we've been overtaken by qiana/ live in a box
with the gong show phil donahue & what's my line
have you nothin ordinary"

she grimaces

"have you no black ribbons"

3)
maybe tallulah will help me/ tho i'ma niggah
maybe faulkner will get out the ground
say cuz i'm a niggah i shd be left alone
maybe appollinaire will have me twirl the
bastille on my tongue
baudelaire assuredly will seduce me
i look like her

but

fame
sits on the typewriter   laughing
she jeers/ shoves/ draws blood actually
my selves have no tongues no voices
some/ no legs/ arms
we are always subject to ambush
fame sends my invalid realities

83/

to islands designed for the criminal
the peculiar/ the socially defective/ the poet
what shall i do there?
have dumas roll me round in a wheel chair
will anna akmatova send me a leftover lover or two
edith piaf has more to do with billie holiday than
we know/ & she's coming
visiting hours are from now til then on saturday
sunday we are free

    4)
my front door's broken/ glass is everywhere
fame's undoing the cobblestones on my street/
my skin with eruptions
i see the sound man when ever i can
i go to flatbush 4 times a week
my self who has no mouth
must be coaxed & pampered
she does not know we are special & has no way
to make arrangements/
she is silent
i am here to translate
noises she makes/ gross stutters
whole words/ acts of aggression
she is my word

when fame sits on my typewriter
i must bind her eyes/ block my ears
she cannot read/ does not understand these realms

i enter/ fame sits undone on the floor
with a trinidadian fan/ the hips of a warm trollop
the voices i am reaching/ for
all my selves who have not yet danced
my selves with no gesture/ no chosen appetite
no throat to scream/ i must grow them out
fame may sit on the typewriter
she can kick & holler/ intimidate me with hysterical
accusations/ but
    my voices with no language
    my dancers with no space
they feed me & carry me
clothed in melody or not
& fame sits by the desk
a dog of suspicious origins
she is you who have no need of me
she is you with mouths history
power & no memory of the unknown
i am the voice of my selves who have not/ learned to speak
my mute & deaf dreams come thru here
my silent daughters
why i speak at all

nappy edges (a cross country sojourn)

    st. louis/ such a colored town/ a whiskey
black space of history & neighborhood/ forever ours/
    to lawrenceville/ where the only road open
to me/ waz cleared by colonial slaves/ whose children never
moved/ never seems like/ mended the torments of the Depression
the stains of demented spittle/ dropped from lips of crystal women/
still makin independence flags/
    from st. louis/ on a halloween's eve to the veiled prophet/
usurpin the mystery of mardi gras/ made it mine tho the queen
waz always fair/ that parade/ of pagan floats & tambourines/
commemoratin me/ unlike the lonely walks wit liberal trick or
treaters/ back to my front door/ bag half empty/
    my face enuf to scare anyone i passed/ a colored kid/
whatta gas

       1) here
            a tree
            wonderin the horizon
            dipped in blues &
            untended bones
            usedta hugs drawls
            rhythm & decency
            here a tree
            waitin to be hanged

    sumner high school/ squat & pale on the corner/ like
our vision/ waz to be vague/ our memory
of the war/ that made us free to be forgotten
becomin paler/ a linear movement from south carolina

to missouri/ freedmen/ landin in jackie wilson's yelp/ daughters of
the manumitted swimmin in tina turner's grinds/ this is chuck
berry's town/ disavowin misega-nation/ in any situation/ & they let
us be/ electric blues & bo diddley's cant/ rockin pneumonia &
boogie-woogie flu/ the slop & short-fried heads/ runnin always to
the river

/ from chambersbourg/ lil italy/ i passed everyday
at the sweet shoppe/ & waz afraid/ the cops raided truants/
regularly/ after dark i wd not be seen/ wit any other colored/
sane/ lovin my life/
in the 'bourg/ seriously expectin to be gnarled/
hey niggah/ over here/
& behind the truck lay five hands claspin chains/
round the trees/ 4 more sucklin steel/

hey niggah/ over here

this is the borderline/
a territorial dispute/

hey/ niggah/

over here/
cars loaded wit families/ fellas from the factory/ one or two
practical nurses/ black/ become our trenches/ some dig into cement
wit elbows/ under engines/ do not be seen/ in yr hometown/ after
sunset we suck up our shadows/

2) i will sit here
my shoulders brace an enormous oak
dreams waddle in my lap
round to miz bertha's where lil richard

gets his process
run backwards to the rosebushes/ a drunk man/ lyin
down the block to the nuns in pink habits
prayin in a pink chapel
my dreams run to meet aunt marie
my dreams draw blood from ol sores
    these stains & scars are mine
      this is my space
        i am not movin

& she bleeds

so her screaming would not give her away
she began to sing
—Susan Griffin

my mother is an indictment
i cry for her
i take back her tail
—Akaua-Lezli Hope

resurrection of the daughter

the family had been ill for some time
quarantined/ socially restricted
to bridge & sunday brunch by the pool
the mother called her daughters twice a day
she saved the son for emergencies
the father drove around a lot
there were no visible scars
under the daughters' biba eyes
lay pain like rachel's/ the rage of zelda
delavallades' pirouettes in stasis
the daughters cd set a formal table
curtsey as if not descendants of slaves
& speak english with no accent at all
they were virgins for a long time
one waz on punishment for a month
cuz she closed her eyes while dancin on the wrong
side of town
mama who came from there/ knew too well
a cheap pleasure cd spell remorse
for an upwardly mobile girl
& the girl learned well/ she paid for her
lovers with her suffering
never knowing some love is due you
she waved her tears in her lover's face
the more there were/ the more they were worth
the son looked down on these things
his women did his laundry & his cooking
but they were not crying
the father waz also not crying he waz with ulcers

& waited on the cliffs
where his daughters' lovers prayed for his demise
dyin to be the heads of a sick household
the lovers of the daughters wrought pain
deception & fear wherever they turned
& the son kept his distance
the mother called him in emergencies/ occurred all the time
the daughters believed they were ugly dumb & dark
like hades/ like mud/ like beetles/ & filth

the mother washed all the time & kept her kitchen
clean
the father wore perfumes/ thot sex a personal decision

a daughter convinced her beauty an aberration
her love a fungus/ her womb a fantasy
left the asylum of her home on a hunch
she wd find someone who cd survive tenderness
she wd feed someone who waz in need of her fruits
she wd gather herself an eldorado of her own makin
a space/ empty of envy/ of hate
she a daughter refused to answer her mother's calls
she refused to believe in the enmity of her sisters
the brother waz callt to see to the emergency
the father bought a new stereo
& she waz last seen in the arms of herself
blushing
having come to herself
in the heat of herself

daughters wait for the wounded to scream themselves
to death
daughters choosin to be women
lick their wounds with their own spit

til they heal

five

her dreams came true & passed
all dreams do
                    n she waz jus a yng thing
wit nothin left   to sleep on/ a
tomorrow imagined
jus come & gone/
                    the hornplayer o.d.'d
                    the dancer waz gay.

her earrings
loopin her shoulders
irregular waz commonplace

                she dreamt a woman waz a tree
                    asymmetrical danglin
uneven motion in the night musk
            (women & oceans repeat symbolically/ never in fact)

& her dreams had passed
the pieces were finished
love happened
applause cheers bows/ encored themselves
it waz all over
                    n she waz jus a yng thing
wit nothin left to conjure
her magic spent on small feats
lil things
a poem here & there   an/arm
some woman burstin   & fleece spun
academic recognition & power

of the spirit
other people's spirits
made her wanna bring em
dream/ s
whoever ya wanna be take it/ in yrself
& rock/ rock/ rrrrockkkk
yr own baby

she waz loved
cuz she freed somebody else from the dark
gave em a yellow rose
all for the dream
& hers
had passed
dead like anybody knows
albert ayler is dead
the lady is dead & bessie . . .
her livin melody killin
itself on avenue c/
nothin left   to/ get up

                        n dance abt
songs were timed/ ended on a cue from a selfish spirit
roamin in the rain

                  that's enuf/ that's enuf
                  dreams are too possible
                  too possible for real/
                  she didnt want but the
                  fullness of her womb
                  in her fingers
                  to be life/ girded with feathers

& silver
masked in orange & apricot smells
she dreamed like a wild thing
& for a minute
jus for a minute
she'd know
words/ brown legs music/ & cloth
uh & lies fists chaos/ & shreds
of dreams/ to be wrapped in
shreds/ of dreams/ to cuddle herself
a wild creature in dangers
of her own makin
(what'll a horn do for ya now/
how much coke cd ya use/ is there
any photo of yrself/ that hasnt turned
to stone)
ahhaaaaaaaaaaaaaaaaaaaaaaaaa/

            dream dreams
         wish wishes
    live a life worth
   reckonin

livin dreams'll make ya crazy
livin dreams'll lead ya to the
end/s of yrself
& her dreams had passed
the indepentisto went to jail
the potter waz impotent
(her poems gathered dust/
audiences craved how she made em/
know another place/ where

95/

they too/ cd saunter unafraid)
but the cats died
the parakeet flew off
the car broke down
a friend raped her
enfamil waz a dirty word
& the dreams passed
she waz left to sleep on scraps
of other times/

she had only wisht for lil things
                    jeweled boxes & rainbows
                    bold men wit tenderness & cruelty
like she waz
always livin dreams
makin somethin into nothin but a vision
& she loved these things
her plants the rockin-chair
any street in san francisco when the fog came in
how the sun picked her up each mornin
she woke in heat
to not a thing she knew
not a dream she cd maneuver
not a glimpse of what she had in store for herself
she had known dream too intimately
for the relationship to continue/
she waz whatta dream waz

nothin made into somethin
breath & blood become a vision

dream dressed up in crepe/ went out on the town
she went on in her life like she tried
not to/ imagine

her dreams had passed
as all dreams do
couched round her eyes

for all my dead & loved ones

(for gail, tracie & viola)

whatever shall i do with my dead
my tombs & mausoleums
these potted plants tended by strangers
over yr eyes   closed
maybe dreamin   dead/ loved
so particularly   i dont know
what to do with you

shall i see you dancin/
hold yr child askin/   what's mammy like
should i sleep with yr husband
who sees yr childself in my memories
yr mother   will she bosom talk me to death with you
pretend she has been no mother
our smokey robinson fantasies set aside
recollections comin to no good end

grandma/ grandma
must i ride with yr daughters to sit
in the cemetery on sunny days/ weedin
yr womb/ wdnt it be better if i stayed
in my kitchen/ makin gumbo/ codfish cakes
watchin edge of nite/
rubbin me hands on my apron/ hummin
his eye is on the sparrow
yr photograph at 25 is on my wall
awready you had given yr woman over/
no one wd know you/ only mama is remembered
when waz there more
i shall not lie fondling a dead man's love

bakin apples for a locket jammed with hair from
a head no longer arrogant
but what shall i do
with my dead/ loved so particularly
leavin me/ specifically

some never stop breathin
wantin kisses
some disappear/ slammin the door
bangin the phone
one went off in a VW bus/ another
stole my sleep

i sit here drinkin memories
entertainin ghosts/ longin for arms
no longer warm/ too enchanted
to tend the pulse pushin me on
to go off from you/ my dead & loved ones

when i meet a someone/ i must know
i place you round me like a court of holy seers
if this stranger is to have a space in my life
she must pull yr spirits to her own
for i wander regularly in moments of the dead
if you wd have me speak
you must learn the tongue of my dead & loved ones
i have been left behind
a survivor
holdin out for more

who is setting these priorities?

1.24.78

today the cosmos satellite fell down over uranium city british colum-
bia, canada. with 100 pounds of uranium 235 on board. There were
international secret meetings for months. no one told me.

today it all cda been over.
i wdnt have had to listen to governor turner refuse to pardon the
wilmington 10 cuz he didnt believe the lies the liars recanted/ i wdnt
have to know that 4 or 3 million american women who take the pill
& smoke are 10 times more likely to have heart attacks than women
who dont take the pill or dont smoke.

what in the hell am i sposed to do?

the wilmington 10 are still in jail. there's only one woman's survival
house in brooklyn. i like to fuck. i'm too nervous not to smoke. no
one likes to eat pussy if you wear a diaphragm. there's hundreds of
pounds of uranium circling the earth & nobody told us. there's chlo-
rine in my water. my show just closed. i havta catch a train at 8:00 in
the morning. & i'm gonna have a heart attack sooner than 7 million
other women cause they either dont smoke/ they wanna be preg-
nant/ or they dont fuck.
i am very upset abt all this.

baron empain waz kidnapped in paris today/ by god only knows
who. for 20 million francs. surely 20 million francs cd fix the pill. the
wilmington 10 defense committee cd use 20 million francs/ 20

100/

million francs wd assuage my troubles with rapid transit. i need a cigarette cuz this is just too much for me. plus there are women who actually find sex boring/ me/ i'm gonna have a heart attack.

on becomin successful

'she dont seem afrikan enuf to know bt . . .'
'seeems she's dabblin in ghetto-life . . .'

why dont you go on & integrate a
german-american school in st. louis mo./ 1955/ better yet
why dont ya go on & be a red niggah in a blk school in 1954/
i got it/ try & make one friend at camp in the ozarks in 1957/
crawl thru one a jesse james' caves wit a class of white kids
waitin outside to see the whites of yr eyes/ why dontcha invade
a clique of working-class italians tryin to be protestant in a jewish
community/ & come up a spade/ be a lil too dark/ lips a lil too full/
hair entirely too nappy/ to be beautiful/ be a smart child tryin to be
dumb/ you go meet somebody who wants/ always/ a lil less/ be
cool when yr body says hot & more/ be a mistake in racial integrity/
an error in white folks' most absurd fantasies/ be a blk girl in 1954/
who's not blk enuf to lovinly ignore/ not beautiful enuf to leave
alone/ not smart enuf to move outta the way/ not bitter enuf to die
at a early age/ why dontcha c'mon & live my life for me/ since the
poems aint enuf/ go on & live my life for me/ i didnt want certain
moments at all/ i'd giv em to anybody/

de poems gotta come outta my crotch?

    (with love to & from ishmael reed)

de kings uv ancient inca-land aztec lakes
& mali bush wuz hi-ho silver/ shanghai jack/
garcia gallavante
sometimes shootin sam   dey wuz de empeers
uv de whole civilizations uv de
colored peoples
hi-ho in de cowboy boat
shanghai in de yangtze boat
garcia in a taino roustabout
shootin sam in de slow boat
              down de nile
de kings uv poesie wid ladies at dey feet/
tween dey thighs a peelin pomegranates
    for our laws uv de given word

diviners n soothsayers outta our archetypal pasts
came to dis heah party de othah nite/ met up wid me
n my sierra-brazen colleague uv graceful trapeze lashes
& sequin studded elbows/
               we weren't claimin to be no queens
             courtesans uv note or de fianci uv howard hughes'
        nicaraguan bastard son or nothin special t'all
    cept i was a tolteca goldsmith's daughter
been mistaken for earth-mama n a particularly pubescent
xhosa sprite
but dis heah king hi-ho he say to me/ king hi-ho he say
    i shd make pies n sleep wid
    de consciously fascist man
    cuz he know de way to be
    de same way dey been

103/

50,000 years/ uv dese kings uv poesie n de sepia peoples
still aint free n de kings get drunk
try to pull pussy outa linoleum shadows
or de naivete uv would-be geishas
   i says
     hey yr majesty rustler upstart uv de black mountain pass
i handle my liquor/ open my own doors/ give good head n
   i make poems/ jack
      get to dat

my mama n my daddy wuz craftsmen
in all de places my soul's been nurtured/ i come from de workers
uv de ancient worl'/ i am de elements

&

de king hi-ho fascist man he say:
  'i'm a man, i can beat em'
  'we men/ we can beat em'

& i says
king hi-ho/ de fiersomest scout uv scoundrel energies in de west
dis heah a luv-u-bettah-get-yr-stuff-togethah-poem
from de quick hands uv a smart dancin girl
workin dem same saloons u been drinkin
in/

sheriff yo self yo own horizon/ toots
    i got too many things to do

                to shoot you rodeo-style from b'hind de knee
            wid a diamond-ringed 45
/lisson here cherokee houngan
                        i got my magic covered
            gonna get all up in yr juju-wangol/ tear it up n
toss it in some ol cheyenne burial grounds/ let yr
inca aztec ibo taino mandarin harlemesque salinas grown
bruised ego get some sun/ gotta be healthy on the range/
poem rustlin/ be demandin a quik draw/

no gusts of wind tickle me

i have always wisht it waznt so hot/
tween my legs/
not like i am not sometimes anxious to be
hot/ tween my legs/
but since tween my legs is always hot/
those moments that might be special
were i one of those women with a space
tween their legs/
a triangle/ where the ridge of their
jeans/ meet/ in the top of the thigh
where the leg warmers open up in preparation
for a demi-plie/ if i were one of them
i wd always know/ i'm sure/ when one of the moments
when the heat swells from inside me/
& i am walkin or thinkin with my hips
forward some kinda soothin of this burnin
up/ wd seem more important/ but since my legs
grow like petals/ one thigh on the other/ i
have never a chilled moment in the
crevice of my pelvis/ no gusts of wind
tickle me/ less i am sittin a stride by
the porch/ i cant even getta good surprise
caress/ less i co-operate & shift the leg from
off the other/
it runs in the family/ legs growin thick
& rounded at the top/ tho our ankles are thin
wda swayed many a fella in the gold rush/ right now
i understand the triangle at the top is the
signal of good breedin/ i am still more

interested in the cosmic experience of space
tween the legs/ does that give a woman a greater
sense of freedom/ she cd run fast & not hear her thighs
rustlin/ steada the sweat streamin from tween her legs/ it
might stream from her brow/ tween her bosom/ maybe
if yr legs dont grow/ one top of the other/ you
cd drive in rush hour traffic in the winter & not be
so uncomfortable/ now i know i'ma big girl/
big enuf laurie says to be worth a lot to a slaver
lookin for a breeder or a worker/ but i hadta lose
40 pounds & eat jello for 10 days just to experience
this space tween my legs/ but then/ i waz so sickly
lookin/ & pale & weak/ the space tween my legs
waz like i waz a child/ who hadnt seen her first
blood/ & so what i wanted to find out/ i never did/
cuz i didnt look like no woman just like a child
playin grown/ & i know my bride price wd be higher in
some parts of the continent/ cuz thighs growin on top
each other are like rattlesnake meat/ a delicacy
& quite something/ & when i think bout the difference
of bein wet alla the time/ & bein dry & then bein wet/
i get all hot tween my legs again/

between a dancer & a poet

(for conyus)

she swayed from the barre   taut   in control
her legs hurt mercilessly   she even laughed
while he took notes
              'i wanna love you   like i dance
                   when i hurt   i'm gettin better'
the poet signed his name to lines eclipsin reality
he cdnt catch his breath   the language waz
overpowerin
             'i can love what i understand
                when i dont understand   i worship'
he put his pencil in his pocket & sat
     in the middle of a whimsical circle
the dancer pliéed   she contracted   she sweat
& grew confident in her struggle
to surpass form   transcend calves ankles hips merely
accoutrements   like a music stand

dance is of the spirit   the body   her sacrifice
to dance
        & she pranced before the poet
  leaped
  chaséed   before the poet   she struck
the air waz an impudent lover   &   the dancer
was righteous chosen to conquer space

she panted   she sweat   & her leotard smelled of heat
& woman   & she laughed
while the poet fondled his own cheek
she slid round him   her body   swirled like a cobra-wind

& she located the poet's soul   in space
                         he lost his spirit   in the rush
of her darin   & she screamed
                    'i wanna love you like i dance
                       wild & delicate   reachin for what i do not know
                       i wanna love you all round yr body
                          in-out-of-it   no grounds no floor

                       i wanna love you where i can dance'
& she caressed the air like an ocean fern
       blazin in the pits of ancient sunflowers
   carryin the poet's soul in the blush of her cheeks
his heart lingerin   in her sweat

serious lessons learned

ah haaaa/ beware beware my dear
of rabid dogs/ gusanos wit grenades
drunken maniacs/ jealous women from the south
& cerebral love affairs/ particularly
a lover who doesnt need to see ya cuz he can make you
up so good when yr not there & he's peelin apples
or when yr not there & he's showin pictures of himself in
grade school wit charlie & bubba to this other woman
he never thinks abt when yr there/ beware beware
of men wit a woman in the head as opposed
to by his side or in his arms or in the kitchen
stay away from a man who can hear yr voice as clearly
in yr presence as in yr absence/ he's dangerously
in love wit himself/ & hasn't met you yet
he may have drawn a sketch of yr back fore he
ever saw you/ or a woman in a porno flick wore the same
kinda panties you had on the first night/ or ya cook grits
just like his sister who he usedta make-believe fuck when he
waz seven/ & you probably look exactly like him if he waz
a female/ yes well/ he loves ya
he says/ time doesnt matter/ how much/
go be wit other men/ & stay away for months/ no need to
correspond/ this man's got ya tied up in his fantasies
yr fleshy & independent reality is insignificant
unpredictable/ touch for him is illusion
is all he wants/ a still-photo of ya is his love
forever/ in control/ watch to see
if he likes ya to sit still
be quiet/ so he can/ capture yr energy/ beware beware

he will leave yr kisses & desires between yr legs
walk off smilin/ thinkin of ya/ tell all the fellas
how he loves ya/ call once a month on the full moon/
cuz he loves ya & remembered that night/ he has stopped
ya in time/ which is death/ necrophilia for the
modern colored man/ has only to do wit a cerebratin
love affair/ beware beware of men who love to think
abt ya & start talkin bout the fights when ya
wanna be loved/ or start not understandin english/
quick/ 'love/ whatya mean love'/
  think abt ya all the time
beware my dear beware/ his dreams of ya are like
whips cross yr back/ this love is not for ya
it's for the women in his head/ caught/
dead/ madly in love wit him/ forever/
beware/ beware lovers in search of illusion
have to betray the truth of you

for marian

we come to the border again
smellin of paramaribo & something schwartze
pornographic
emmerich   our ankles wrapped in orange
beads & sweat like anne frank's chin
biberkoff's surprise at his friend's death

"we dont know you where you come from
so these guns escort you out of our land"

our scent waz jasmine like our mouths wide
we had to go back where we came from
schwartze
but the music survived
the music waz hubcaps   nappy heads
arrogant like a niggah's sposed to be
the music even bought us a drink
for wanting to love enuf to breathe/
all the dying here   emmerich
we shd march it thru the sky
surround it with men still tremblin
on the lynchin tree   sweep up the bloated bodies
of all of us in the rivers
pour gin on em   set it a fire
leave it singing sadness in chicago
we smell of paramaribo
schwartze
we cant be stopped

our lips too thick
the air too strong

(moérs, germany/ during A.I.R. concert/
fred hopkins, steve mccall & henry threadgill)

with no immediate cause

every 3 minutes a woman is beaten
every five minutes a
woman is raped/ every ten minutes
a lil girl is molested
yet i rode the subway today
i sat next to an old man who
may have beaten his old wife
3 minutes ago or 3 days/ 30 years ago
he might have sodomized his
daughter but i sat there
cuz the young men on the train
might beat some young women
later in the day or tomorrow
i might not shut my door fast
enuf/ push hard enuf
every 3 minutes it happens
some woman's innocence
rushes to her cheeks/ pours from her mouth
like the betsy wetsy dolls have been torn
apart/ their mouths
mensis red & split/ every
three minutes a shoulder
is jammed through plaster & the oven door/
chairs push thru the rib cage/ hot water or
boiling sperm decorate her body
i rode the subway today
& bought a paper from a
man who might
have held his old lady onto

a hot pressing iron/ i dont know
maybe he catches lil girls in the
park & rips open their behinds
with steel rods/ i cdnt decide
what he might have done i only
know every 3 minutes
every 5 minutes every 10 minutes/ so
i bought the paper
looking for the announcement
there has to be an announcement
of the women's bodies found
yesterday/ the missing little girl
i sat in a restaurant with my
paper looking for the announcement
a yng man served me coffee
i wondered did he pour the boiling
coffee/ on the woman cuz she waz stupid/
did he put the infant girl/ in
the coffee pot/ with the boiling coffee/ cuz she cried too much
what exactly did he do with hot coffee
i looked for the announcement
the discovery/ of the dismembered
woman's body/ the
victims have not all been
identified/ today they are
naked & dead/ refuse to
testify/ one girl out of 10's not
coherent/ i took the coffee
& spit it up/ i found an

announcement/ not the woman's
bloated body in the river/ floating
not the child bleeding in the
59th street corridor/ not the baby
broken on the floor/
    "there is some concern
    that alleged battered women
    might start to murder their
    husbands & lovers with no
    immediate cause"
i spit up   i vomit   i am screaming
we all have immediate cause
every 3 minutes
every 5 minutes
every 10 minutes
every day
women's bodies are found
in alleys & bedrooms/ at the top of the stairs
before i ride the subway/ buy a paper/ drink
coffee/ i must know/
have you hurt a woman today
did you beat a woman today
throw a child cross a room
    are the lil girl's panties
    in yr pocket
did you hurt a woman today

i have to ask these obscene questions

116/

the authorities require me to
establish
immediate cause

every three minutes
every five minutes
every ten minutes
every day

the suspect is black & in his early 20's

(in the bay area in the spring of 1974
the black community waz besieged by the
hysteria created by the coincidental
S.L.A. Patricia Hearst kidnapping & bank
robbery & the alleged 'Zebra' killings.
everyday for three months the media
announced 'the suspect is black & in his
early twenties.' every day every one of us
(women included) under 6 ft., brown black beige,
waz subject to suspicion of wanton murder.
wanton oppression the likes of which
suggest the trips to tule lake, pinochet's
stadium, the days of blood in buenos aires.)

i always hated bigger
thomas   he treated bessie
sooooo bad   a brown girl
trying to sing thru bitter winter young
& accustomed to brutes   bessie
waz a secondary murder   an effect
dying with her in the vacant bldg
bigger thomas was no longer a man to me
bigger thomas was a thug   with no love
til i remembered   who
mary dalton   waz
a hincty smart aleck rich white girl

troubled bout the colored problem & the jews
concerned bout bringin some excitement to her
life/ mary dalton cost bessie   a possible lover

118/

a gig in a segregated tavern   maybe
a new dress   her grandchildren
it waz mary dalton   her drunken ashes
her wanton charred bones sent thousands of
bullets looking for a blk boy
any one nigger wd do   the suspect is black
& in his early 20's
the suspect is our sons
again prey to whims & caprices of
grande dame white ladies
with tears & curses for their fathers
white ladies whose consciences drive them to
come to us   drive them to join us
patricia hearst alias mary dalton
      has joined us
has paraded her debutante
bred body in fronta the 7 headed serpent
machine gun in hand she wants the people
to embrace her soft white fingers/ to save us
from death/ the compulsion of fascists to kill
the suspect is black & in his early 20's
      listen
mary dalton has risen from the dead
      mary dalton has risen from the dead/
she yearns for all bigger's sons & daughters
            to climb into the furnace
with her   her ashes   her burnt blonde hair
is all   that is real   patricia hearst   alias tania
how dare you present yrself to us

years ago   before i waz born
a man i hated all my life   a thug   a po blk boy
        burned you in yr father's furnace
                    burned you to ashes
                    burned you to ashes
                        you have nothin for us
you are ashes
you are dry bones
you are the bringin of death to our sons
            the suspect is black & always in his early 20's

oakland in february

everyday/ now
somebody is gettin it on
to death   like   everyday   now
somebody is dyin   like
yesterday   a blk god   fell
blank   in the schoolhouse door
slidin in his own blood   bullets force him
push his breath   his comin/ & goin

       "i am the blk god
      i seek revenge gainst the devils
         the white devils"

yesterday/ the blk god
held his elbow round a sister's neck
his fingers tearin a child's shoulder
hostages/ the peons
      a woman & child
everyday   now
somebody is dyin   everyday somebody
gettin it on to death
late model chryslers dark & gas-glutted
sneak past in bright afternoon
         "killers lurk on the corners"

is what they say
everybody stays in   nobody asks questions
      "was it him/ the blk god/
      carried away/ a maniac/"
like they say

  121/

everyday now   somebody is getting it on
to death/ i avoid lookin in yr face
the blk god screamin/ killin/   everyday/
we be gettin it on/ to get back/ we lie
rather than betray our sons/ on some street/ battered/ blood-washed
everyday now   somebody is
gettin it on to death
murder   my first thot each mornin

& she bleeds

to speak/   a test of silence
bein heard
a woman in shadows echoes her mama scramblin eggs
the search for the ribbon/ the indelible woman spit
of herself
to make
to share
to scream in the center of stars
on the edge of the tenderloin/ in the mission
to giggle to love/ to tug at breezes
police cars   violators boozers n children
to give up
throw away bein held
in the knot of what is not
her own
our language   is tactile
colored & wet
our tongues speak
these words
we dance
these words
sing em like we mean it/
      do it to em stuff drag punch & cruise it
to em/ live it/ the poem/
my visions are my own
my truth no less violent than necessary
to make
my daughters'
dreams as real as mensis

whispers with the unicorn

i never could decide
between the arts & zoology . . .
in the middle of a vision
i ride the unicorn through
the midtown tunnel
i refuse to speak the English language.

—Jessica Hagedorn

ecstacies do not occur often enough

—Anais Nin

i live in music

i live in music
is this where you live
i live here in music
i live on c♯ street
my friend lives on b♭ avenue
do you live here in music
sound
falls round me like rain on other folks
saxophones wet my face
cold as winter in st. louis
hot like peppers i rub on my lips
thinkin they waz lilies
i got 15 trumpets where other women got hips
& a upright bass for both sides of my heart
i walk round in a piano like somebody
else/ be walkin on the earth
i live in music
        live in it
            wash in it
i cd even smell it
wear sound on my fingers
sound falls   so fulla music
ya cd make a river where yr arm is &
hold yrself
            hold yrself in a music

tropical dance

    (for mercedes baptista)

en bahia women wrap
cloth like sun flowers
round their heads move
like soft coast waves in
velvet rufflin gusts of
wind
    the samba
ripples every muscle
quivers wakes up to rhythms
dances flirts
mercilessly pink coral earrings
taunt at shoulder's length
one hand motion is the midnight
secret in-out in-out in-out
hips laugh uhuhuh
ankles-buoyant guide toes
kneadin the earth small
winsome streets brown
bodies sing silver
bracelets tinklin
en bahia women move
graciously still swayin
still tall swayin graciously
ripplin the samba swayin
limbs like water-falls
still gracious flowers burst
intricate rhythms of sunsets
swayin clouds gracious still
sway embracin the skies

en bahia
women
samba

advice

people keep tellin me to put my feet on the ground
i get mad & scream/ there is no ground
only shit pieces from dogs horses & men who dont live
anywhere/ they tell me think straight & make myself
somethin/ i shout & sigh/ i am a poet/ i write poems/
i make words/ cartwheel & somersault down pages
outta my mouth come visions distilled like bootleg
whiskey/ i am like a radio but i am a channel of my own
i keep sayin i do this/ & people keep askin what am i gonna do/
what in the hell is goin on?

did somebody roll over the library witta atomic truck
did hitler really burn all the books/ it's true
nobody in the united states can read or understand
english anymore/ i must have been the last survivor of
a crew from mars/ this is where someone in brown cacky comes
to arrest me & green x-ray lights come outta my eyes & i
can leap over skyscrapers & fly into the night/ i can be
sure no one will find me cuz i am invisible to
ordinary human beings in the u.s.a./ there are no poets
who go to their unemployment officer/ sayin i wanna put
down my profession as 'poet'/ they are sure to send you to
another office/ the one for aid to totally dependent persons/

people keep tellin me these are hard times/ what are you gonna be
doin ten years from now/ what in the hell do you think/ i
am gonna be writin poems/ i will have poems/ inchin up the
walls of the lincoln tunnel/ i am gonna feed my children poems on
rye bread with horseradish/ i am gonna send my mailman off

with a poem for his wagon/ give my doctor a poem for his heart/
i am a poet/ i am not a part-time poet/ i am not an amateur
poet/ i dont even know what that person cd be/ whoever that
is authorizing poetry as an avocation/ is a fraud/
put yr own feet on the ground/ writers dont have to plan
another existence forever to live schizophrenically/ to
be jane doe & medea in one body/
i have had it/ i am not goin to grow up to be somethin else
i am goin to be ol & grey wizened & wise as aunt mamie/
i am gonna write poems til i die & when i have gotten outta
this body i am gonna hang round in the wind & knock over
everybody who got their feet on the ground/ i'ma let you
run wild/ & leave a poem or two with king kong
in his aeroplane to drop pieces of poems
so you all will haveta come together/ just to figure out/
how you got so far away/ so far away from words
however/ did you capture language/ is a free thing.

elegance in the extreme

   (for cecil taylor)

elegance in the extreme
gives style to the hours
of coaxing warmth outta
no where

elegant hoodlums
elegant intellectuals
elegant ornithologists
elegant botanists

but elegance in the extreme helps most
the stranger who hesitates
to give what there is
for fear of unleashing madness
which   is sometimes
uninvolved in contemporary mores
archetypal realities or graciousness

in the absence of extreme elegance
madness can set right in like
a burnin gauloise on japanese silk
though highly cultured
even the silk must ask
how to burn up discreetly

one more poem for dolphy

it's not like the old days
when unicorns cd only have virgins
is now a time for men & women
who love & fight & free move
see this is a city time
wit changes rattlin
      congas trample in our dreams
sometimes on a off hour
we cd sing but unicorns
have a hard time on market street/ hard
to find a lover for a horn like one of them
less he make it a flute/
           blow his pain
         outta touch
          breathe his life
              thru our kiss
a melody to   caress
unicorn masqueradin as a bass clarinet
wit everyone/ i love/ eric
it's not like in the ol days
   we are all innocence
       as you come near
        more ourselves
yr breath quiets us
      let's us be/ no holds
someone more to cherish/ someone never taken/
comin always as air

cross oceans into my heart

all i know is his name/ is james or jim/ shortened
somebody very very black & tall
so-phisticated for that time/ fore the war & he waznt
born here/ either/ born in paris/ carried to detroit when he
waz five/ a french-speakin niggah in detroit/ say 1926/

& he waz intense

a rich colored boy in the Depression
a pouter/ a brooder/ who took a wife
who didnt like just men in ohhhh/ maybe 1943

he hadda boat floatin in the detroit river
served in korea/ gotta be a physician/ did abortions
for girls bout my age when i waz in high school/

i know he owned bars by wharfs & up from transient
hotels/ he dealt smack/ & never hadda son
i always wanted to meet him

when he waz in college he usedta pay his friends
    to look after him while he waz out/
        he was suicidal

    (my daddy & his girl rode in the backseat
    of the newest & hottest car in nashville
    on the way to where fletcher henderson might
    be/ some all colored spot/ & he/ jim/ wd
    buy lotsa whiskey/ & listen/ & seem to be

133/

treatin daddy & his girl/ who waz poor/
but they were workin/ really/ makin sure/
jim didnt kill everyone/ thinkin he waz
mad music/ another kinda dangerous miles
davis/ an impersonal assassin of his own love/
so daddy & his girl rode in the front seat/
on the way back from anywhere/ & jim lay
molten in his back seat)
& he wd stay in his room til his parents left campus or
til his wife's lover left town

(everybody knew abt her/ that she liked
to touch women's legs/ & mouths/ that
there waz nothin cd be done/ cuz she
had connections/ & he waz so sharp &
he took her/ & the sorority took her/ &
there waz nothin cd be done/ cuz she waz
beautiful/ & then there he waz/ & wd
you mess wid him who is anger/ a
malignant fury/ in his glance/ when
someone wanted to say/ what everybody
knew abt her/ & did leave them alone/
& how cd he not know/ & if he did know
it must be he is really a foreigner/ not
a whole man himself/ to have a woman so/
a woman/ so fulla beauty/ she shared when
a breeze fell from her hands/ he never
left her)
i waited & waited to meet him

134/

& i have just found out how i waz in love
how i waz in love wid this man who has died
& i never knew him to touch
i never saw a picture/ but not far from me
not far from me/
never far from me/ i've kept a lover
who waznt all-american who didn't believe & wdnt straighten
up to standard & i've loved him

i've loved him
in my own way/ in my own men/ sometimes hateful/
sometimes subtle like fog in high skies & sun/
i cherished your not believin/
i loved yr bitterness & hankered after
space in you where jim's fury swept round like
cab calloway's band in '3—D'/ where you are outta control/
where you cannot touch/ or you wd kill me/ & somebody else
who loved you

i never even saw a picture
& i've loved him all my life
he is all my insanity
anyone who loves me will understand

my father is a retired magician

(for ifa, p.t., & bisa)

my father is a retired magician
which accounts for my irregular behavior
everythin comes outta magic hats
or bottles wit no bottoms & parakeets
are as easy to get as a couple a rabbits
or 3 fifty cent pieces/ 1958

my daddy retired from magic & took
up another trade cuz this friend of mine
from the 3rd grade asked to be made white
on the spot

what cd any self-respectin colored american magician
do wit such a outlandish request/ cept
put all them razzamatazz hocus pocus zippity-do-dah
thingamajigs away   cuz
colored chirren believin in magic
waz becomin politically dangerous for the race
& waznt nobody gonna be made white
on the spot   just
from a clap of my daddy's hands

& the reason i'm so peculiar's
cuz i been studyin up on my daddy's technique
& everythin i do is magic these days
& it's very colored
very now you see it/ now you
dont mess wit me
                    i come from a family of retired

sorcerers/ active houngans & pennyante fortune tellers
wit 41 million spirits critturs & celestial bodies
on our side

             i'll listen to yr problems
             help wit yr career   yr lover   yr wanderin spouse
             make yr grandma's stay in heaven more gratifyin
             ease yr mother thru menopause & show yr son
             how to clean his room

YES YES YES   3 wishes is all you get
        scarlet ribbons for yr hair
           benwa balls via hong kong
             a miniature of machu picchu

all things are possible
but aint no colored magician in her right mind
gonna make you   white
     i mean
           this is blk magic
you lookin at
             & i'm fixin you up good/ fixin you up good n colored
& you gonna be colored all yr life
& you gonna love it/ bein colored/ all yr life/ colored & love it
love it/ bein colored/

SPELL#7 FROM UPNORTH-OUTWEST GEECHEE JIBARA QUIK MAGIC TRANCE
MANUAL FOR TECHNOLOGICALLY STRESSED THIRD WORLD PEOPLE

ego

(for june jordan)

use of the word
                    i
is totally unjustifiable so
we have no way of distinguishin
i from whatever we are unless
somethin else is goin on that
mistakes the dynamic of us
for mine or the treasure of
ours for theirs,
we talkin abt sharin or isn't
one all encompassin ego enough to
satisfy you/ us is all we got 'n
won't one i ever succeed in
vanquishin we/ the strength
and beauty of whatever we is
will singularly outdo an i/
effortlessly with grace
          an i is clumsiness/ narrow
          sight and sniffin round like
          a hound for where we are/ cuz i
          is lonely and lonely is different
          from the space we allow each other
          for ours/ lonely is close and dark
          and i
have known a solo self
in languishin funny houses long
enough to know that
we is the answer

flying-song

1)
i want to say these things to you
mostly cuz yr not here
if you were here   we wd kiss
rub all denim thru

i speak to you a lot/ when i'm alone

i want to tell you
i cannot stop smoking kools
forget the militia in panama
all brown & bald in gestapo boots
paradise has her own ugliness
the man on the boat from dusseldorf chasing me
to dance with a 'colored'/ the first in his
life/ this my april in the north
atlantic/ to say what of
chateaubriand/ une mousse chocolate
at dusk the sea is sultry
we are not her lovers & she treats us so.

2)
did you know i have so many secrets
i believe are yrs/ what of me
i need you to have & still cant imagine
you ever thot i wanted you to see the posters
in rio/ guerilleros' faces taped to steel
remind me of our struggle/ how
we merge in our eccentricity

139/

this penchant for the right to live
this penchant for the right to love
peter tosh awready said 'everybody's talkin
abt peace/ i talkin abt justice'
our kiss is desperate
long awaited/ known immediately/
unequivocal/ & not enuf/ tupac amaruo knew what to do

    3)
i imagine you in guadalajara
on the back of a donkey
the 3 yr old pick pocket will seduce you
this is not the first time i've swallowed
bad white wine/ i've been betrayed by
escalators before/ no one knows you've
planted here/ no one knows
you find wine tricklin from my body/ our
champagne still squirts from my braids
even now i am not empty

such things i wd say
tho cecil taylor long ago past quevy station
in the cemetery there
i smelled my self in soil/ bitter & french
dark & falling apart in my hands

    4)
i wd say to you
a marimba might civilize me

a fashion fair in bangkok   suffocate my sense of style
jessica swears the yng men in manila
dance well but have no minds
i want to hold you in this
so you might know
what i bring you

my mouth is full & broad
my tongue cluttered with syllables & desire
this has not come out straight
so many days uprooted
each time i fly
i know again
memory & desire are relentless
when yr not here to talk to
i speak my most precious
lay out the mystery/ the devastation
my honor/

i cant even catch yr eye
so i trace the skies with
     these hidden things
ces choses perdues
that you might find me/ in the night
when i am flying

chicago in sanfrancisco & you/ me/ waait/ love is musik/ touch me
like sounds/ chicago on my shoulder/ yr hand/ is now a kiss

   (for thulani & joseph)

i get inspired in the middle of the nite
when you make love to me

after i've held you & kissed you & felt alla that
i get inspired get cherished/ free of pain/
not knowin anymore what is dream/ but is love like they are singin
to me odawalla/ reeese & the smooth ones/ here where you kissed
me/ & i feel you/ i cd make it up again/ but we're already musik
joseph roscoe lester don & malachi/ i hear em in our sweat
& nobody is speakin/ but the rhythms are chicago/ melody on the
loose/ when you make love to me/ i shout like the colors on joseph's
face/ am bound to air like roscoe's horn/ like the 'cards' are stacked
in our favor/ one slight brown thing bip-bloo-dah-shi-doop-bleeeeha-
uh/ refusin false romance/
                          when it waznt what ya wanted/ or who ya thot
waz comin/ but it waz real tenderness/ cant lie
                                          i remember
cards always gotta have a full deck/ gotta have a woman/ queen of
spades/ like malachi slipped in wit the grace of nefertiti or eubie
blake/ this aint what we expected
                          THE ART ENSEMBLE OF CHICAGO
but it waz colored/ waz truth/ waz gotta rhythm/ like you feel to
me

i really wanted to be a waitress to serve em in a negress way/ push
my waist thru a tight black skirt & amble like a alto in bird's mouth/
a secret/ too sweet to hold tears/ i wanted musik/ & they brought
love in a million tones/ & i am not the same anymore/ not any
more/ you wanted a sigh/ i made like a flute/ i pull/ i ease back &
splee-bah-wah-she-do-the-do-tso/ ring like a new reed cant stoppa

142/

cherokee/ a jackson in yr house/ congliptis/ all round/
the art ensemble cd make ya love more/ cd make you love more/

chocolaté or miz t. in all her silver/ dont inspire me like i get in-
spired when you hold me in chicago harmonies/ & we waltz like va-
grants/ get up/ signal the release of pain/ scream/ sing/ then sigh/
groan/ sound/ make the sound that kisses me/ one note/ you/ make
me melody/ is/ is musik/ uh true uh/ yes/ musik is the least love
shd bring ya/ most ya'll ever have/ you/ yes/ musik/ you/ let love
musik you/ you kiss me like the sound/ we/ let love/ is the musik/
watch us dance/ & let the musik/ you take it all/ get the musik/ let
the musik love you/ close/ like silence

marine intrusion

    (for pepo & nashira)

when a woman can walk down gold street
feeling like she's moved to atlantis/ when the mine's
been closed a hundred years & the only gold is music
seepin thru fog/ it's what we call a marine intrusion
interlopin visions & lost deities
findin the way home/ like thieves/ cuz we dont recognize
what's sacred anymore

women in big hats wit lilies behind their ears
women in blk & white scarves dance on stairways wit bougainvillea
& clouds/ men in jeans & honest faces/
                                music offers solace/
offers some kinda way to reach out/ to ring
bells on gold street/ not tin pan alley/ but montezuma's
preciousness/
         a marine intrusion natural as tides/
learnin to pray/ to give more of yrself/ than ya think ya have
diggin below the bottom of what's possible/ & so clean
like a expensive gangster/ a tibetan shaman's prophecy
marine intrusion/ like wind/ like winds make fires
make dust swirl/ make us catch ourselves/ fly against
our will/ til we like it/ til we know we waz meant to soar/
to be free
        in truth
more
ourselves & music
       like a voice we cannot speak in
     a voice to move thru
marine intrusion's a meteorological phenomenon

like rain

like rain & sun like c'mon   c'mon
like felipe says
        "the consequence of bein real"
                        unpredictable as the weather
sure as the sun risin
                the sweet come-uppance of risk

if ya wear a lotus in yr hair
                it'll fly wid the horn

                    marine intrusion movin soft/ marine intrusion
cant hurt ya/ dontcha wanna be music/
            dontcha wanna be
                        daybreak & ease inta fog
a cosmic event
sound
& rain/

yeah. like rain.

an invitation to my friends

you have to come with me
to this place where music
is to hear my song some
times i forget & leave my
tune in the corner of the
closet under all the dirty
clothes in this place the
music asks me where i've
been how i've been singin
lately i leave my self in
all the wrong hands with
human beins who think they
can be stars givin off
sunlight while they slink
in sewers & have babies w/out
no african names
                  even the children
                  are breast fed
i have no illusions that
AM radio will quickly sweep
them toward the 5 & 10 where
they will grow old & gnarled
in the head like that talkative
man who looks after frankenstein
if you were to come with me
to this place where music is
tenderly involved in undoin
our masks i will be able to
smile & answer that i have
no children of my own but

i like small human beins
very much 'n yes i can get
to my house w/out assistance
though one time i forgot
where i lived & made the
taxi-man go round 'n round
the block three times before
i cd identify my dwellin
this place where music always
asks for me i discovered a lot
of other people who talk w/out
mouths who listen to what i say
by watchin my jewelry dance

there is somethin
sacred abt bein invited to bring
yrself to someone's song if you
come w/ me next time music
will ask us both to come into
ourselves 'n be our own children
who forget what we were told
rememberin only to be what we are

in
ourselves
there
is
the
world
& in this place where music stays

147/

you can let yrself in or out
wherever you have to go there
are vehicles available for earthy
poets usually grow beyond the rushes
& when you leave yrself at home
burglars 'n daylight thieves
pounce on you & sell yr skin
at cut-rates on 10th avenue
so come with me to this place
i know where music expects me
& when she finds me
       i am bathed in the ocean's breath
         & the soft glory of my laughter